We believe in one God, the Father, the Almighty, maker of heaven and earth, of all things visible and invisible; and in one Lord, Jesus Christ, the only-begotten Son of God, who was begotten of the Father before all ages, Light from Light, True God from True God, begotten, not made, having the same being as the Father, through whom all things came to be; who for us human beings and for our salvation came down from heaven, and was incarnate from the Holy Spirit and the Virgin Mary and became human, and was crucified also for us under Pontius Pilate, and suffered and was buried, and rose again on the third day according to the Scriptures, and ascended into heaven, and sits at the right hand of the Father, and shall come again in glory to judge the living and the dead, of whose kingdom there shall be no end; and in the Holy Spirit, the Lord and Giver of Life, who proceeds from the Father, who with the Father and Son together is worshiped and co-glorified; who has spoken through the prophets; in one, holy, catholic, and apostolic church. We confess one baptism for the forgiveness of sins; we look for the resurrection of the dead and the life of the age to come. Amen.

"Phil Cary's commentary on the Nicene Creed exhibits two virtues—clarity and brevity, which entail a third—usefulness. Here is a truly inviting introduction to the faith once delivered to the saints in baptism and continuously declared throughout the world in the church's confession."

—Scott R. Swain,
president and James Woodrow Hassell Professor of Systematic Theology,
Reformed Theological Seminary

"To sum up the Christian faith in just over 200 pages is no small task. To do so while unpacking the technical language of one of Christianity's most ancient creeds is almost unfathomable. Yet Phillip Cary has managed to pull it off. His little handbook on the Nicene Creed manages to be erudite, insightful, and interesting—all at once. Phrase by phrase he unpacks the meaning of words that many find mind-numbing, using language that is both interesting and colloquial. Laced with Scripture, this book will tickle your imagination while expanding your vocabulary and strengthening your faith in the only begotten Son of the Father who came down from heaven to bring life to a dying world."

—Harold L. Senkbeil,
author of *The Care of Souls*

"With characteristically lively prose, engaging style, and endearing wit, Phil Cary takes us on a stroll through the history of heated debates over the nature of Christian faith-claims that forged the creeds. He lays out for us the theological reasoning at the heart of the conciliar decisions and their ramifications for spiritual health. Meaty yet accessible, this volume will help worshipers who recite the creed to understand better what they confess. Likewise, it will challenge those who are skeptical of the function and origin of creeds, nudging them to reexamine their assumptions. Highly recommended for adults of all ages and stages, for parish study groups and personal learning alike."

—Kathryn Greene-McCreight,
affiliate priest, Christ Church, New Haven;
spiritual director, Annand Program, Yale Divinity School

"Phillip Cary's book is so much more than a phrase-by-phrase commentary on the Nicene Creed; it is my new favorite go-to book for systematic theology. It is careful and scholarly, yet in Cary's style. ... Several books have been written recently highlighting the importance of the creeds and confessions. And for good reason! The church across denominational lines is seriously adrift on a big sea looking for the right place to drop its anchor. Carl Truman famously wrote that 'Scripture is the norming norm, creeds are the normed norm.' He's right, and what the Triune God has done for his creation is summarized in the Nicene Creed. Phillip Cary beautifully unwraps this treasure. This can be read as a daily devotional or by small groups, or it will be a library resource that pastors grab first in their preparations to preach and teach."

—THE REV'D CANON CHUCK COLLINS,
director, Center for Reformation Anglicanism

"For over a thousand years the church across the globe confessed the Nicene Creed together. To be a Christian meant worshiping the Trinity of the Scriptures, a Trinity our church fathers described in the creed with orthodox clarity over against the threat of heresy. How strange—indeed, how sad—to admit that many Christians today have never read or confessed the Nicene Creed. Some have never even heard of the Nicene Creed. Phillip Cary's book is a harvest in a time of famine. With a precision that does not forfeit accessibility, Cary not only explains each word in the Nicene Creed, but he summons the church today to link arms with brothers and sisters of yesterday to confess a Trinity apart from which we have no Christianity. My earnest prayer is that every Christian reads this book!"

—MATTHEW BARRETT,
author of *Simply Trinity*; associate professor of
Christian Theology at Midwestern Baptist Theological Seminary

THE NICENE CREED

An Introduction

THE NICENE CREED

An Introduction

Phillip Cary

LEXHAM PRESS

The Nicene Creed: An Introduction

Lexham Press, 1313 Commercial St., Bellingham, WA 98225
LexhamPress.com

Print ISBN 9781683596332
Digital ISBN 9781683596349
Library of Congress Control Number 2022937322

Lexham Editorial: Todd Hains, Abigail Salinger, Danielle Thevenaz, Mandi Newell
Cover Design: Joshua Hunt, Brittany Schrock
Typesetting: Abigail Stocker

In gratitude to the pastors and people
of the Church of the Good Samaritan, Paoli,
and St. Mark's Church, Philadelphia

Contents

Article 1: God the Father

Article 2, Part 1: The Eternal Son of God

Article 2, Part 2: God Incarnate

Article 3: The Holy Spirit

Prayer

When the Spirit of truth comes,
    he will guide you into all truth.
He will glorify me,
    for he will take what is mine
    and declare it to you.
All that the Father has is mine.   *John 16:13–15*

Glory to God in the highest,
and peace to his people on earth.

Lord God, heavenly King,
almighty God and Father,
we worship you,
we give you thanks,
we praise you for your glory.

LORD JESUS CHRIST, only Son of the Father,
Lord God, Lamb of God,
you take away the sin of the world:
have mercy on us;
you are seated at the right hand of the Father:
receive our prayer.

FOR YOU ALONE are the Holy One,
you alone are the Lord,
you alone are the Most High,
Jesus Christ,
with the Holy Spirit,
in the glory of God the Father.
Amen.

FATHER IN HEAVEN, who at the baptism of Jesus in the River Jordan did proclaim him your beloved Son and anoint him with the Holy Spirit: Grant that all who are baptized into his name may walk in newness of life and boldly confess him as Lord and Savior; who with you and the Holy Spirit lives and reigns, one God, in glory everlasting. *Amen.*

Introduction

The Historical Setting

𝕿HE NICENE CREED originated because ancient Christians were appalled. A teacher in one of the most influential churches in the world was trying to get them to speak of Christ and say things like "there was once when he was not" and "he came to be out of nothing." They had good reason to be appalled. Christians worship Jesus Christ as Lord, exalted at the right hand of God the Father Almighty. To say "there was once when he was not" would be to say that he is not eternal like God the Father—that he came into being from non-existence just like all God's creatures. That would mean he is not really God at all, but one of the things God made. To say this would be to say that what Christians have been doing all along, worshiping Jesus as Lord, is the kind of thing pagans do: worshiping something that is not fully, truly, ultimately God. The Nicene Creed was written to say *no*, in the strongest possible terms, to that kind of Christian paganism.

It said *no* by saying *yes* to who God really is, and who Jesus is. It states the essentials of Christian faith in God the Father and his eternal Son, Jesus our Lord, and it adds some essentials about the Holy Spirit as well. And sometimes it says who God is by saying what he has done to make us who *we* are: God's creatures whom he raises from death to everlasting life in Christ. So the Creed is a fundamental statement of the gospel of Jesus Christ, who is God in the flesh coming down from heaven for us and our salvation, so that we may share in his kingdom that has no end.

The *no* is important because of the *yes*. To say *no* is to draw a boundary and say: We're not going there, because that's not who Christ is. False teaching about who Christ is leads us away from faith in the real Christ and gives us a bogus substitute. It

means preaching a different gospel from the one that comes
to us from our Lord's apostles, which is why the apostle Paul
goes so far as to say: Let anyone who teaches differently be
anathema, accursed (Galatians 1:9). Heeding the apostle, the
Council of Nicaea in the year 325 composed a creed that is the
precursor to the one this book studies, and added anathemas—
solemn curses against anyone who teaches things like "there
was once when he was not" or "he came to be out of nothing."
It did not name Arius, the man who taught this, because its
purpose, like Paul's, was not to condemn a particular man but
to exclude what he taught. Arius was always free to change his
mind, to repent, to submit to the judgment of the Council and
teach the same truth. But real heretics are stubborn (you can't
be a heretic just by being mistaken; you have to persist in teaching your mistake to the church even after being corrected), and
eventually the doctrine that took shape in opposition to the
Council of Nicaea came to be known as Arianism, one of the
most famous heresies in the history of the church.

But this book is not about a heresy but about the truth:
the gospel of Jesus Christ taught by the Creed that grew out
of the faith of Nicaea. It's a book for Christians who want to

understand their own faith better, and thus to grow in the knowledge of God, by learning what the ancient teachers of the Nicene faith had to give us.

𝕿HE COUNCIL OF NICAEA, after which the Nicene Creed is named, was a gathering of bishops in AD 325. They met in the city of Nicaea in Asia Minor, which is now the town of Iznik in Turkey. It is a little more than fifty miles as the crow flies from Istanbul, the city that used to be called Constantinople back when it was the capital of the Eastern Roman Empire. Rome itself was defeated a century or so after the Council of Nicaea and the Western Roman Empire gradually disintegrated, but the Eastern Empire remained for another thousand years and became what is known as the Byzantine Empire—after Byzantium, the earlier name for Constantinople. "Constantinople" means "the city of Constantine," the Roman emperor who made it his capital in 330 and who had also called the bishops to come to the Council at Nicaea in 325.

Nicaea came to be recognized as the first ecumenical council, from the Greek noun *oikoumene*, or *ecumene* in Latin, meaning "the whole inhabited world." An ecumenical council is a council for the church throughout the world, the church of the *ecumene*. This was a new idea, but meeting in councils was not. Christian bishops, the leaders of local churches, had been meeting for years in regional councils or synods (from *synodos*, which is just the Greek word for "council"). This was an important way of keeping order in the churches and of keeping the faith. A bishop had the job of preserving the faith as it was handed down in the church of his town since the time of its founding. The name for this handing down in Latin is *traditio*, from which we get the word "tradition." It was a handing down that began in some places, such as Jerusalem and Rome and Antioch, in the earliest days of the Christianity, before the New Testament was written. If there was a serious discrepancy in teaching or church practice between one town and another, the bishops could meet in a synod to straighten things out. The Council of Jerusalem, for example, met to straighten out disputes about how the churches growing out of the missionary work of the church of Antioch were handling things (Acts 15:1–35). In that case, the burning question was how to incorporate believers in Christ who were not Jewish into the fellowship of the church. In this case, at Nicaea, the question was how to exclude the teaching of Arius from churches throughout the world.

The most important way the bishops did that was to produce a confession of the Christian faith—which is what a creed is. Prior to this time, creeds were handed down orally rather than written, as people coming to Christ were taught some form of confession to affirm when they were baptized. It was a way of saying what they were committing themselves to as they joined the Body of Christ. The confession of faith that we now know as the Apostles' Creed, for example, took shape originally in Rome as an oral baptismal confession.[1] Each town had its own traditional confession, handed down through generations of bishops, with many small variations. But they all followed a threefold pattern, so that everyone in the *ecumene* was baptized in the name of the Father, the Son, and the Holy Spirit, as our Lord commanded (Matthew 28:19). What evidently happened at Nicaea is that one of these unwritten local confessions was adapted, with some additions directed specifically against Arius' teaching, to provide a single creed for the whole *ecumene*.

THE CREED PRESENTED in this book is the most widely-used confession of faith in the Christian world. It is not the original

Creed of Nicaea in 325 but an expanded confession formulated at the Council of Constantinople in 381 and officially accepted as a statement of the Nicene faith at the Council of Chalcedon in 451.[2] In the interests of historical accuracy, scholars often give it a long name, like the "Niceno-Constantinopolitan Creed," but I will use the more familiar name "Nicene Creed," which accords with the reason it was accepted by the church throughout the world: it is a fuller way of confessing the same faith as the Council of Nicaea. Thus for the purposes of this book, as well as in the ordinary usage of the church, the label "Nicene Creed" designates a different text from "the Creed of Nicaea." Along with a number of small differences, the Nicene Creed omits some things in the Creed of Nicaea, including the anathemas, and adds a good deal to what is said about the Holy Spirit. The result is an expanded confession of the faith of Nicaea, and as such it has come to be accepted as *the* ecumenical Creed, the confession of the Nicene faith of the whole *ecumene*, and is incorporated into the regular worship of the vast majority of Christians around the globe, including Eastern Orthodox, Roman Catholics, and most Protestants who use a regular liturgy.

It is worth saying a bit more about the unity and diversity within what we can now call the *ecumenical* church, the church of the *ecumene* that agrees in confessing the Nicene faith. It is the church that deserves to be called orthodox (small "o") because it teaches the right faith and worship (*orthe doxa* in Greek). It is also catholic (small "c"), meaning "universal" (*katholikos* in Greek). And it is evangelical (small "e") because it is the church of the gospel (*euangelion* in Greek). In the lower-case sense of these words, the one holy church of God, which the Creed teaches us to honor as the Body of Christ and the work of the Holy Spirit, is orthodox, catholic, evangelical, and ecumenical, and its faith is the faith of Nicaea.

The diversity within the one ecumenical church, which ought not to divide it, can be distinguished by names with capital letters. We will need to mark the distinction between orthodox (small "o"), which embraces the whole Nicene *ecumene*, and the Orthodox (capital "O"), including Greek Orthodox, Russian Orthodox, Armenian Orthodox, and many others, all grouped under the heading "Eastern Orthodox," whose heritage can be traced back to the Eastern Roman Empire, where the dominant language was Greek. And we must likewise mark the distinction between catholic (small "c"), a term we will meet in the Creed itself to designate the whole church, and Roman Catholics (capital "C") who are Christians in full communion with the Pope, who is the bishop of Rome. Their heritage goes back to the Western Roman Empire, where the dominant language was Latin. Very early on, there was a standard Latin translation of the Nicene Creed that ended up—as we shall see—with a few differences from the Greek version, one of which is trivial, another interesting, and the third tragic. Protestants are heirs of this Western tradition, and most translations of the Nicene Creed used in the Protestant churches have their roots in the ancient Latin translation. The Latin Creed is still with us, familiar to lovers of church music by composers such as Palestrina, Bach, and Mozart.

T HE TRANSLATION OF the Creed I have made for purposes of this book does not have exactly the same wording as any version used in the churches, for unfortunately there is no one standard translation of the Nicene Creed in English. I assume that readers will continue to say the Creed in the version they're accustomed to using on Sundays—I certainly hope so, for the opportunity to confess the faith together in worship is one of the great blessings of the Creed, and not something to tamper with. But because there are so many versions, some of which go back hundreds of years and use English that is no longer familiar, I will often need to comment on alternative translations and old wording that might be confusing. In my own translation I have tried to stay as close as possible to the original Greek.[3] But I have also commented on the standard Latin translation when it diverges from the Greek, for this often explains variations in the English versions, giving us words like "consubstantial" and phrases like "was made man."

To organize the phrase-by-phrase commentary, I have divided the Creed into its three "articles," which is a technical term (from which we get the phrase "an article of faith") for the parts of the Creed devoted to the Father, the Son, and the Holy Spirit. In addition, it is convenient to divide the second article into two parts, the first centered on the divinity of the Lord Jesus and the second on his humanity.

As you may have noticed already, a great deal of this book focuses on words and their history. For the Creed consists of words that are much older than any of us who now say them. A richer and more accurate understanding of these words is therefore a way of arriving at a deeper understanding of our own faith, which we share with those who have confessed the

Creed over the centuries of the Christian tradition. For with them we too have been given one Lord, one faith, and one baptism.

Because the words are old, they have layers. One aim of this book is to give you access to these layers, so that when you say a word like "incarnate," you will hear beneath it the Latin word *carnem* and will think "flesh." And then you can tune your ears to the way the word "flesh" echoes down the hallways and passages of Scripture and into the Creed, as well as into the language we use in church services. I will assume readers of this book are familiar with the Bible but not necessarily with the traditions of Christian theology, so I will spend a good deal of time on words like "incarnation," which for theologians are very commonplace, but which for many churchgoers, I have found, are unnecessarily mysterious and easily misunderstood, because the words have never been explained to them. Getting our ears more fully tuned to hear these words gets us more deeply immersed in the richness of Christian worship.

It is another aim of this book to open doors to further study, and for that purpose I will often introduce theological terms that are not found in the Creed itself, but that have been used in the Christian tradition to expound the Nicene faith. I will frequently be dwelling on technical terms that theologians use without explanation—terms that I think are genuinely helpful not just for those studying the technicalities of theology but for ordinary Christians who want to understand their own faith. I will be very happy if this book serves some readers as a gateway to theological studies.

The book will also devote a great deal of attention to the apostolic roots of the Nicene faith as found in Scripture. The aim in this is to show biblical Christians how the Creed gives words to what they already believe, so that they can hear these words as gospel, the story of our God. In Martin Luther's terms, the Nicene Creed gives us gospel rather than law, because it is not telling us what to do but telling us what God has done for us and our salvation—all the things we cannot do to save ourselves, transform our lives, and make ourselves good Christians, for they are things that only God can do. The good news is that in Christ, God has done these things, and by his life-giving Spirit he has made them ours. The Nicene Creed is a blessing and a joy, for it is a confession of faith in this good news.

THE NICENE CREED

(In a close literal translation, with alternative versions in brackets)

We believe [I believe]

in one God,
the Father, the Almighty,
maker of heaven and earth,
of all things visible and invisible;

and in one Lord,
Jesus Christ,
the only-begotten Son of God,
who was begotten of the Father before all ages,
[God from God,]
Light from Light,
True God from True God,
begotten, not made,
having the same being as the Father,
through whom all things came to be;

who for us human beings and for our salvation
came down from heaven,
and was incarnate
from the Holy Spirit
and the Virgin Mary

and became human,
and was crucified also for us under Pontius Pilate,
and suffered
and was buried,
and rose again on the third day according to the Scriptures,
and ascended into heaven,
and sits at the right hand of the Father,
and shall come again in glory
to judge the living and the dead,
of whose kingdom there shall be no end;

and in the Holy Spirit,
the Lord and Giver of Life,
who proceeds from the Father
[and from the Son],
who with the Father and Son together is worshiped and co-glorified,
who has spoken through the prophets;
in one, holy, catholic, and apostolic church.
We confess one baptism for the forgiveness of sins;
we look for the resurrection of the dead
and the life of the age to come.

men.

WE BELIEVE [I BELIEVE]

$\mathfrak{T}$HE INTERESTING DIFFERENCE between the Greek and the Latin versions of the Creed, which was mentioned in the Introduction, is found right here in the first word: the Greek-speakers in the Eastern Roman Empire said "we" and the Latin-speakers in the West said "I."[4] This is in fact how we got the term "creed," from the Latin word, *credo*—a one-word way of saying, "I believe." Turn it into a noun, "the *Credo*," and you have a standard term for the Creed. The standard Greek term, on the other hand, was simply "the faith," *he pistis*. So in this sense the Nicene Creed *is* the Nicene faith. To repeat the Creed aloud is to confess the faith, in a double sense of the term: it is to give utterance to the Christian faith in the words of "the faith," which is the Creed.

Another ancient term for the Creed, surprisingly enough, is "symbol" (from the Latin *symbolum*, derived from the Greek *symbolon*). It is a word with many meanings. To this day, the English word "symbol" can be used to designate a creed, and if you see a book in the theology section of the library on "Symbolics," it is probably an old study of creeds and confessions.

Exactly why *symbolum* was used to designate a creed or confession of faith needs an explanation, which will also help us see why the West said "I believe." In ordinary Latin, *symbolum* could be used to mean a sign or token, such as a password or the sign and countersign used by soldiers to recognize each other. Instead of saying "Halt! Who goes there?" a sentry in the dark of night might give the first half of a password as a sign, and his fellow soldier completes the password with a countersign ("O Susanna!" / "Oh, don't you cry for me!"), thus identifying himself as one who belongs to the same army. Another meaning of *symbolum* was an oath or pledge of allegiance used when a soldier was inducted into the army. The practice of baptism worked like this in the early church. To be baptized was like joining Christ's army—an unusual army in which you did not kill but might well be killed, bearing witness as a martyr—and your baptismal confession was the pledge by which you were identified, as if by a kind of password, when you signed up.[5]

The actual baptismal ceremony looked a bit like giving a sign and countersign. It involved three questions, which could be as short as "Do you believe in God, the Father Almighty?" and "Do you believe in Jesus Christ and his cross?" and "Do you believe in the Holy Spirit?"[6] Usually the questions were longer, and could be quite similar to the Nicene Creed; for example: "Do you believe in Christ Jesus, the Son of God, who was born by the Holy Spirit from the Virgin Mary, who was crucified under Pontius Pilate and died, and rose again on the third day alive from the dead, and ascended into the heavens, and sat at the right hand of the Father, and will come to judge the living and the dead?"[7] In any case, the response to each question was the same: "I believe," after which the person was immersed in water. This threefold immersion was Christian baptism, and the question-and-answer was the *symbolum*, the baptismal sign and counter-sign of the Christian faith. Turn the question-and-answer into a confession that we can all say together, and you get a creed.

The Creed is the faith we *confess*, which means simply that we say it aloud. The act of uttering something aloud makes a difference, as when we confess our sins rather than hide them. To confess *the faith* is to make what we believe into something shared, public, and recognizable, not just a fleeting thought in the heart. The baptismal confession makes us members of Christ's army, and to this day there are places where this confession can get you killed. So confession is more than expression. It is not just saying what is in our heart; it is joining a community and sharing its dangers and tasks as well as its blessings. When we say "I believe" in our baptism or "we believe" in a Sunday liturgy, we are making a commitment that is a pledge of allegiance, joining us to other believers around the world in the Body of Christ, some of whom are bound to get into trouble for keeping this commitment.

Hence even when Christians in the West begin the Creed with the words, "I believe," this is not just an individual expression of faith but a commitment to the faith of a community, the Body of Christ which the individual has joined in baptism.

Some Western churches have in fact now switched back to the Greek version, saying "We believe." Yet in an important sense, "I believe" is actually the older form of confession, being used in baptisms long before Nicaea. "We believe" was a new way of confessing the faith, reflecting a new setting. Instead of a baptismal confession, it was a conciliar confession. The Nicene Creed begins with "we believe" because it originated as the confession of a council, a gathering of bishops presenting what they believed and taught as the faith of the whole ecumenical church, to be confessed together. This is also why it was eventually incorporated into the eucharistic liturgies of the churches, both East and West.

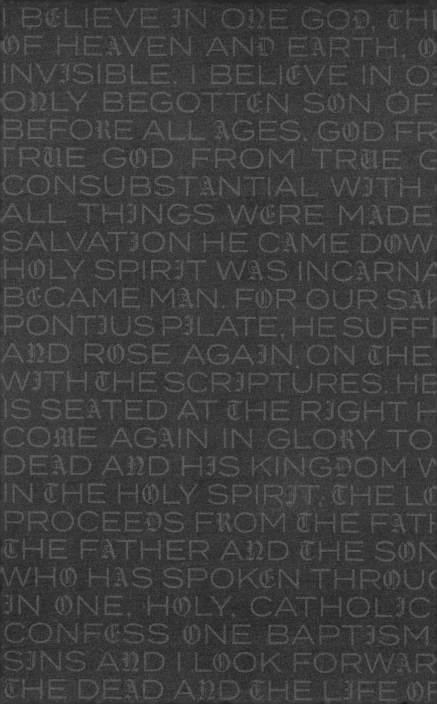

ARTICLE 1

GOD THE FATHER

In One God, the Father, the Almighty

T HE CREED BEGINS by using familiar language, common in ancient philosophy as well as pagan mythology, but it soon proceeds to do something unprecedented with this language. "Father Almighty" was a term well-known among pagans. It appears frequently, for example, in the Roman epic poem the *Aeneid*, to designate Jupiter, the king of the mythological gods on Mount Olympus. It turns out that Jupiter is hardly what Christians would call almighty, as he is easily frustrated by the scheming of other gods and the problems of mortals. Certainly, creating heaven and earth is well beyond his power—not to mention ruling it in justice and wisdom, which is an especially prominent aspect of the Greek term here, *Pantokrator*, which literally means "Ruler over all things." The Creed is talking not just about power but about how God our Father governs all things—which, as we shall see, means that his Son, a crucified man, is king forever.

We should also bear in mind that belief in one God was by no means unique to Christians and Jews. Sophisticated pagans, such as the philosophers Plato, Aristotle, and Plotinus, had much to say about a unique First Principle that was eternal and divine, but which was not a personal being like Jupiter. Aristotle actually called this principle "God," while Plato called it "the Good," and Plotinus made it the source of all things. Christians who studied philosophy found a good deal to like in this kind of philosophy, and it became common in Christian theology to speak of God as the First Principle, the supreme Good which is the source of all things. But in confessing the Creed, ancient Christians were using this shared language, "one God," to say something more specific and biblical, which only starts to be clear when we come to see why, in the second article of the Creed, we will hear of Jesus as the "one Lord."

Maker of Heaven and Earth

THIS PHRASE LANDS us, of course, right at the beginning of the Bible, when God created heaven and earth (Genesis 1:1). Scripture uses the phrase "heaven and earth" to designate the whole creation from top to bottom. Together, heaven above and earth beneath are all the things that exist, other than the God who made them all.

In Genesis 1, however, the word "heaven" is used in a rather limited sense. It refers to the visible heavens we can see above us, populated by the stars, the moon, and the sun—just as the sea is populated by fish, the air by birds, and the earth by creeping things and cattle. Elsewhere the Bible speaks of a highest heaven that is above the heavens we see, calling it "the heaven of heavens."[8] This is where God is enthroned above the visible heavens, because "his majesty is above earth and heaven" (Psalm 148:13). It is a place beyond the places of the visible universe—not a place we can travel to (no spaceship could ever take us there) for it is where our Lord Jesus Christ is enthroned at the right hand of God the Father, surrounded by the unending praise and gladness of the angels and archangels and all the host of heaven. Because this is high above the visible heavens, a different dimension from any place we could ever see, the Creed must go beyond all visible things in order to speak of the fullness of what God has created.

OF ALL THINGS VISIBLE
AND INVISIBLE

The NEWER TRANSLATION that many churches use, "seen and unseen," is not quite as precise as "visible and invisible," because what the Creed speaks of here is two realms of the creation, and the invisible realm is not just something we haven't seen but something we cannot ever see with our physical eyes. It is the realm of angels, both the blessed angels in heaven and the demons, who are fallen angels cast out of heaven (Revelation 12:7–9).

This phrase lands us in the letter to the Colossians, which teaches us that the creation of all things is the work of Christ, by whom "all things were created, in heaven and on earth, visible and invisible" (Colossians 1:16). So before we are done with the first article of the Creed, we find ourselves describing the Creator of all things, God the Father, by using a biblical description of Christ. This is utterly appropriate, for the Lord Jesus Christ is the one *through whom* God brought all things into being, as we shall see in the second article. One of the main purposes of the Nicene Creed is to make the distinction between Creator and creature absolutely clear, and to put our Lord Jesus on the Creator side of it.[9]

The phrase "all things," as the Creed uses it, includes the whole creation but not the Creator. The Creator of all things cannot be counted as one thing among others, as if he belonged on the list of "all things." If you could make such a list, God would not be on it, for he is the source of the list and everything on it, and is not confined within it—any more than an author is confined within the pages of a book he's writing. You can call him the Supreme Being, but only insofar as he is the source of all being, the author of it all, not just one being among others.

With that in mind, we can properly understand what the Creed is saying when it contrasts visible and invisible. For the passage in Colossians has more to say about "all things … visible and invisible," which were created by Christ, "whether thrones or dominions or rulers or authorities," all of which "were created through him and for him" (Colossians 1:16). This is a list of the powers of highest heaven, where the throne of God is above and beyond the whole visible universe. It is not a supernatural realm in which Christ is one member among others (a favorite fantasy of the heretics known as gnostics). It is the invisible realm that was created by him, through him, and for him, using the same almighty power in which he is one with the Father and the Holy Spirit, and thus is the one Creator of all things.

It is worth saying something also about lesser items on the list of "all things," not so glorious as the creatures in the highest heaven. By saying "all things" are made by God, the Creed steers us away from certain materialist mistakes. First of all, there is no material out of which God made things. God created all things out of nothing, as taught in the Christian doctrine of *creatio ex nihilo* (which is simply Latin for "creation out of nothing"). This is why the original Creed of Nicaea cursed the idea that Christ "came to be out of nothing," which would make him a creature. Second, God himself is not a material being. That is to say, there is no material or stuff out of which he is made. Every kind of material that exists is God's creature, an item on the list of "all things." Its being is dependent on God, not the other way round. So unlike material things, God does not need anything to be made out of. There is nothing God is composed of, and he has no parts. This becomes an important point in the doctrine of the Trinity, which, as we shall see, is not a doctrine about God having three parts.

God is not made out of anything because God is not made at all. He is, as the Christian theological tradition likes to say, "uncreated." So there is a clear answer to the child's question, "If God created everything, then who created God?" The answer is that no one created God, for God cannot possibly be created. It is of the very *essence* of God (a concept we will get to shortly) to be uncreated. He is the Creator, not a creature. That is what we must say so long as we are discussing the first article of the Creed. Something new shows up, of course, when the second article gets to the baby born of Mary, who is God incarnate.

Finally, at the lowest level of all, if it can be called that, there is what is so debased that it never manages to get on the list of "all things." *Evil* is not among the things God created, so it never has an existence of its own. Evil takes place when the good things God created go wrong, when they are broken or deformed or corrupted, like a ruined house or a diseased animal, a community at war with itself or a soul corrupted by sin. The great power of evil is entirely derived—stolen, we could say—from the power that rightly belongs to God's good creatures: the power of a good house to stand firm in wind and rain, the power of an animal to live and grow and procreate, the power of human beings to live with one another in friendship, and the power of an individual human being to participate with neighbors in the glory of worshiping the one true God. All the powers given to things by the Creator can be ruined and corrupted in their own distinctive way, and the more powerful the creature, the greater and more powerful the ruin that results. This explains the sense in which Satan is both the greatest and the worst of God's creatures.[10]

So there is an answer to that other question children ask: Did God create the devil? The devil is indeed God's good creation, belonging on the list of "all things" that God has made. But he is a good thing that has been corrupted, spoiled, and ruined by his own misuse of the power of free will given to him when he was created—a good power that makes possible an intensity of love and joy beyond the capacity of lesser creatures, but which in its corrupted state is only the power to spread misery, wickedness, falsehood, and death.

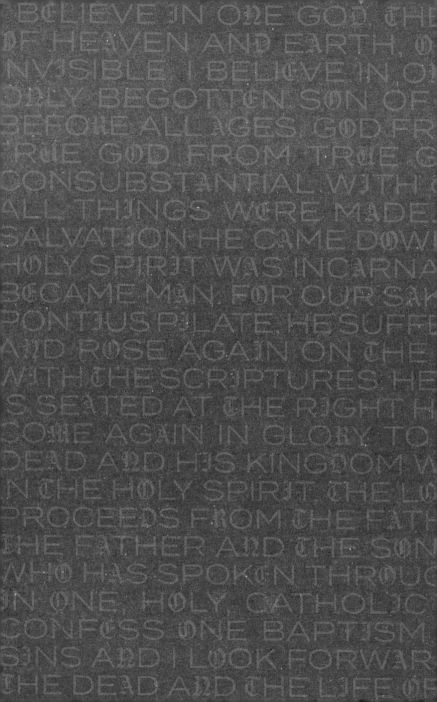

ARTICLE 2, PART 1

THE ETERNAL SON OF GOD

And in One Lord

Ｊ N THE SECOND article of the Creed we come to what is distinctive about Christian faith, different from every other belief in God. The phrase "one God" in the first article must be paired with the phrase "one Lord" here. These words set up a distinctively biblical field of force like the poles of a magnet, each of which attracts more words to itself, gathering its own characteristic vocabulary. The word "Father," for example, belongs strictly to the pole of the first article, whereas the word "God" is less precise and particular, and will be used not only in the first article but also in the second article, describing Christ as "true God from true God." Meanwhile the word "Lord," although it can also be used of the Father and of the Holy Spirit, has been pulled in by the second article and firmly attached to the name of Jesus. When Christians say "our Lord," they mean Jesus. So when the Creed says "one Lord," it proceeds to speak of Jesus Christ, just as when it spoke of "one God," it proceeded to speak of the Father.

In this the Creed follows a widespread pattern in the New Testament, in which the words "God" and "Father" go together, and the way to say that Jesus is God is to call him "Lord," applying to him the sacred Name of the LORD, the God of Israel. This is the fundamental way that Scripture testifies to us that Jesus is one and the same God as the Father: he is none other than the LORD. So the pattern of naming here needs to be discussed in detail.

Start with the Name of the LORD. Spelled with four capital letters, this English word is used in many Bible translations to indicate the Name of the God of Israel, without actually putting it in writing. You will sometimes encounter a version of the Name written with four letters, YHWH, without any vowels, so that it is not really possible to pronounce it. The four Hebrew letters this represents are called the Tetragrammaton (which is just a Greek term for "four letters"). In other words, the Name of God is so important that it has a name of its own: the Greeks call it the Tetragrammaton, but the Jews call it *HaShem*, Hebrew for "the Name," which is the custom that I am following here.

The Name needs a name, because no one now can say it. Nobody quite knows what vowels belong in it to make it pronounceable, for ancient Hebrew was written without vowels, so we don't have original biblical texts with the vowels written in to tell us how the Name was pronounced. By the time vowels were included in Hebrew texts, centuries after the New Testament, pious Jews had long ceased pronouncing the Name at all, for it was regarded as too sacred to utter aloud. Scholars have made educated guesses about what the vowels were, but those who respect the living traditions of Judaism do not try to make the Name pronounceable by writing it out with vowels included. (It is worth noting that one failed attempt to make the Name pronounceable, based on an outdated transliteration of the Tetragrammaton, JHVH, resulted in an English word that has appeared in a number of hymns, such as "Guide me, O Thou Great J—." According to modern scholarship, however, this is certainly not how the Name was pronounced.)

In addition to the term *HaShem*, there is another important way that Jews to this day avoid saying the Name. When they read Scripture aloud in the synagogue, for example, and come upon the Tetragrammaton written in the text, they do not try to pronounce it but instead say *Adonai*, which is the Hebrew word for "Lord." Most English Bibles follow this practice by using the word LORD with four capital letters to render the Name, while rendering the Hebrew word *Adonai* by using the word "Lord" with only one capital letter. Thus in Psalm 16:2, "I say to the LORD, 'You are my Lord,' " we have first the sacred Name, then the ordinary Hebrew word for "Lord." Keeping these two words straight is necessary for understanding the Old Testament, for when the God of Israel declares, "I am the LORD," he is not claiming to be master or lord or ruler; he is announcing his name. He says so in Isaiah 42:8: "I am the LORD; that is my name; my glory I give to no other." Likewise, when he passes before Moses saying "the LORD, the LORD, a God merciful and gracious, slow to anger, and abounding in steadfast love and faithfulness" (Exodus 34:6), he is proclaiming his Name (Exodus 33:19). And thus also, before giving Moses the Ten Commandments, he says who it is that is giving this law to Israel: "I am the LORD your God, who brought you out of the land of Egypt, out of the house of slavery" (Exodus 20:2).

Greek-speaking Jews in the ancient world followed a similar practice when they translated the Bible from Hebrew, and the writers of the New Testament did likewise. Instead of writing a version of the Name, they used the Greek word *kyrios* (sometimes transliterated *kurios*), which means "Lord." This is the word used in the Creed for the Lord Jesus. It is familiar to many English speakers (with the ending changed slightly) from the opening prayer of some Sunday services, often set to music: "Lord have mercy," *Kyrie eleison.* The Creed, with its confession of "one Lord, Jesus Christ," is telling us that it is not a different lord when the prayer proceeds to say, "Christ have mercy," *Christe eleison.*

The primal Christian confession of faith in the New Testament attributes the Name of the LORD to Jesus, saying *Kyrios Iesous*, "Jesus is Lord." For example, when the apostle Paul wants to explain why those who confess with their mouths that Jesus is Lord are saved (Romans 10:9–10), he quotes the Old Testament saying, "Everyone who calls on the name of the LORD shall be saved" (Joel 2:32, quoted in Romans 10:13). According to the teaching of the apostle, therefore, confessing

Jesus as Lord is the same thing as calling on the Name of the LORD, the God of Israel. So "Jesus is Lord" means that Jesus is the LORD. The sacred Name of the God of Israel rightly belongs to him. That is the heart of Christian faith and is therefore the heart of the Creed.

This is of course an extraordinarily bold thing to say. To anyone who does not accept the Nicene faith, it must look like idolatry. It means calling a man by the name of God and honoring him with the same worship given to the Creator of all things. But this is evidently what Christians were doing from the very first.[11] The earliest Christian writing we have is a hymn quoted by the apostle Paul, which looks forward to the day when "every knee should bow ... and every tongue confess that Jesus Christ is Lord" (Philippians 2:10–11). This is plainly meant to indicate the fulfillment of the vow made by the LORD himself in Isaiah 45:23: "To me every knee shall bow, every tongue shall swear allegiance." Thus to worship Jesus, according to this ancient hymn, is to worship the God of Israel, the LORD, who says, "My glory I give to no other" (Isaiah 42:8). To glorify Jesus is therefore not to give glory to anyone other than the LORD; it is in fact worship that is for "the glory of God the Father" (Philippians 2:11), as the hymn adds in conclusion.

The confession that Jesus is LORD thus goes along with prayer to God the Father in this fundamental biblical pattern of naming. Perhaps it began when the disciples came to Jesus asking how to pray. How can anyone call on the LORD when his Name must not be spoken? Jesus' answer, of course, was: "When you pray, say, 'Father, hallowed be your Name …'" (Luke 11:1–2). So Christians call upon the God of Israel by calling him Father, and thus they hallow the Name by refraining from saying it, just like Jesus' Jewish disciples. "Hallow" is just an old English word for "make holy" or "sanctify," which is to say, to set apart. We hallow the Name of the LORD by praying as our Lord Jesus taught us, setting apart the Name by not saying it, and instead calling God "Father," as the Creed does.

The resulting double pattern of naming is found throughout the New Testament, as for example in the letters that begin by blessing their readers in the name of "God our Father and the Lord Jesus Christ" (Romans 1:7, 1 Corinthians 1:3, Galatians 1:3, etc.), and the phrase "the God and Father of our Lord Jesus Christ" (2 Corinthians 1:3, Ephesians 1:3, 1 Peter 1:3).

The fundamental pattern is simple: God is Father and Jesus is Lord. Perhaps the most striking example, and the one that is most important in shaping the Creed, is 1 Corinthians 8:6, which pairs the two phrases "one God" and "one Lord." After acknowledging that the world has in it many lords and many things that are called gods (1 Corinthians 8:5), the apostle contrasts the idolatry of the world with the faith of Christians:

> Yet for us there is one God, the Father,
> from whom are all things and for whom we exist,
> and one Lord, Jesus Christ,
> through whom are all things and through whom
>   we exist.

It is clear that if we want to confess the one God of Christian faith, not confusing him with the many gods and lords of this world and the "almighty fathers" of empty mythology, we will need to keep the magnetic connection between "one God, the Father" and "one Lord, Jesus Christ" steadily in view. When we confess in the Nicene faith that God is the Father Almighty, we have in view first of all that he is eternally the Father of the only-begotten Son of God, Jesus Christ our Lord, and second, that he is our Father, for we are adopted sons and daughters of the one God, whom we call "Our Father" according to the words given to us in the Lord's Prayer (Matthew 6:9).

Finally, it should also be clear that by confessing faith in one Lord, Jesus Christ, we are turning our back on paganism but not on Judaism. The one Lord we worship is the same one Israel names in the great confession of faith given to it in Deuteronomy 6:4: "Hear O Israel, the LORD our God, the LORD is one." The extraordinary boldness with which Paul identifies this one LORD with the Lord Jesus makes the Christian Creed dependent on this ancient and fundamental Jewish confession of faith, which has always been and continues to be the biblical faith.

JESUS

H E IS NAMED Jesus, so the angel said, because he will save his people from their sins (Matthew 1:21). The name is a variation, in the ancient language of Aramaic, of the name "Joshua," meaning "the LORD saves." In its Hebrew version, it includes an abbreviated form of the sacred Name, as is common in many ancient Israelite names. The English version of the name is derived from the way it appears in the Greek New Testament, *Iesous*, which is exactly the same as the name for "Joshua" in the ancient Greek translation of the Old Testament.

In other words, Jesus is the new Joshua—indeed the true Joshua, the one who truly saves his people from all their enemies, including sin and death, and brings them into the promised land of the kingdom of God, where the LORD will establish a place for his Name forever. He is one of many people named "Jesus" in first-century Israel, as we know from the historian Josephus. It seems they were hoping for a new Joshua, one who would re-conquer the promised land and expel the pagans who were occupying it, so that "we should be saved from our enemies and from the hand of all who hate us," as the father of John the Baptist says (Luke 1:71). Hence the crowd gathering to greet Jesus as he enters the holy city welcomes him like a conquering hero, crying, "Blessed is the King who comes in the name of the LORD" (Luke 19:38). And they are right. In a few years the temple itself shall be thrown down, not one stone left upon another (Luke 21:6), and Jerusalem made desolate (Luke 21:20); but in Jesus Christ himself, in his own body raised from the dead, the LORD will rebuild the temple in three days (John 2:19–22) and thus establish a place for his Name in a kingdom that will have no end.

This true Joshua is long expected, and yet different from what was expected. His life, his coming, and his kingdom are the fulfillment of Israel's expectation in a way that is beyond expectation. They wanted a new Joshua who would free them from their enemies. They got the true Joshua who saves all humanity from its enemies.

CHRIST

WE TEND TO use this word now as a name, but it was originally a title. Pilate got the sense of it accurately enough when he had "King of the Jews" posted on the cross. The English word "Christ" comes from a Greek word meaning "to anoint," to daub or smear with oil in a ceremonial action that could also be called *unction*. The Hebrew word for it turns into the English word "Messiah," meaning the "anointed one." For in ancient Israel kings were made not by crowning them but by anointing them with consecrated oil. Priests were anointed as well, which is why the particular kind of Messiah that Jesus is can be distinguished from other kinds by the title, "Son of

David." He is a royal rather than priestly messiah, for he is the descendant of King David and thus the rightful heir of the throne of Israel. So Christ, the Messiah who is the Son of David, is indeed the King of the Jews.

It turns out this is also why lots of people were wondering if Jesus was claiming to be the Son of God (Luke 22:70). The high priest at his trial, for example, demanded: "Tell us if you are the Christ, the Son of God" (Matthew 26:63). He wasn't asking if Jesus claimed to be God (that was beyond his wildest imagination), but was remembering how God spoke about the Son of David, the Messiah or Christ, as his own Son. For when the LORD gave David a son to be the next anointed king, he promised that the throne of his kingdom would be established forever, and he added: "I will be to him a father, and he shall be to me a son" (2 Samuel 7:14). The Son of David, in other words, is the Son of God. He is adopted by the LORD as his own. This is true of the whole royal lineage of David, whose throne is everlasting. Hence, in what is evidently part of a liturgy for anointing the king of Israel, the LORD declares to David's descendant and successor: "You are my Son; today I have begotten you" (Psalm 2:7). This is a declaration of adoption. It is as if the LORD were saying to the world: "On the day he is enthroned, the anointed king of Israel becomes my own son, part of an everlasting lineage that will reign forever."

This declaration is a covenantal promise to David and to all Israel about the meaning of Christ the Messiah, the King of Israel who is the Son of David. He is the Son of God, as the high priest said, as well as King of the Jews, as Pilate said. And yet it turns out he is Son of God and King in a far deeper way than either of them guessed. The New Testament quotes this piece of liturgy and presents it as the word of God the Father spoken to his eternal and only natural-born Son (Hebrews 1:5). "You are my Son," as the New Testament and the Creed understand it, means something much more than adoption. And "Today I have begotten you" has a meaning that goes deeper than any of the days of creation, as we are about to see.

The Only-Begotten
Son of God

T HE NEWER TRANSLATION, "the only Son of God," captures one important meaning of the Greek term used here,
monogenes. It was a word that could designate an only son
(Luke 9:38) or an only daughter (Luke 8:42). But the word
means more than "only." It consists of the Greek word for "only"
(*monos*) plus an adjective that could refer broadly to origination (as in *genesis* and *generation*), or more specifically to
the birth of people and animals. If English had a single word,
"onlyborn," that functioned just like "firstborn," then that would
be about the perfect word to translate *monogenes*. It suggests

not just an only son but an only natural-born son. Its use in the Creed accommodates the fact that God has many adopted sons and daughters, who all have him as their own Father because of what has been accomplished by his only natural-born son, Jesus Christ. We are daughters and sons of God by grace of adoption, as he is the Son of God by nature.

The traditional translation, "only-begotten," looks forward to what the Creed says next. Begetting is what precedes birth. "To beget" is a familiar activity, but nowadays it is not a familiar word. Readers of the King James Bible will remember how it is repeated in the lists of "begats," which trace the lineage from fathers to sons in passages like Genesis 5 and Matthew 1, where Abraham begat Isaac, and Isaac begat Jacob, and so forth. Taken literally, the word describes how a son originates from a father, or a calf from a bull, or a colt from a stallion. It is how any new animal comes from its male parent. Fathers beget, mothers conceive, and children are born, not just in the human species but throughout the animal kingdom.

So what does the Creed mean when it speaks of a Son of God who is begotten? This takes us far beyond the literal and familiar, and into the middle of ancient Christian controversies about who Christ is.

Who Was Begotten of the Father before All Ages

ᴡITH THIS PHRASE we find ourselves at the center of the mystery of God. It is language that points paradoxically at what is beyond all language, as it speaks of the origination of the eternal Son of God from his Father. Unlike God the Father, the Son does have an origin: he is "of the Father," where "of" has the sense of "from," one thing coming *from* another. The Father is unbegotten, unoriginated, not derived from any source or origin—the only language we have for this is negative, a denial of the Father originating from anything. The Son is different: he does have an origin, for he comes *from* the Father. But of his origination too we must speak mostly in negative terms, saying what it is not.

The Son does not originate through a process taking place in time. There is no "before" and "after" in his begetting, like when a father on earth begets a son. For there was a time before the earthly father begat his son, a time when the son did not yet exist. There is no such thing in the eternal begetting of the Son of God. He does not come to be in time, for his being is as eternal as the Father's. Yet he does have an origin, and that origin is his Father. The Father is eternally Father, which is to say he has always had a Son, for he is *eternally* the origin of his Son. Hence the Council of Nicaea fiercely rejected the notion that we could speak of the only-begotten Son of God and say "there was once when he was not."

The Nicene Creed speaks of the origination of the Son of God by saying that he was begotten "before all ages." The ages are all the times of the world, including every moment that passes and gives way to the next. Time is a kind of succession, as one age replaces another, like the reign of one king succeeding another, son after father. The eternal origination of the Son of God is before all that, before any succession of one thing after another—which is to say, before there is any *before* and *after* in time. So the "before" in "before all ages" is not like the way that one time comes before another. It is paradoxical language pointing at something we don't really understand or know how to say.

What we are talking about here is incomprehensible, beyond understanding—as well as ineffable, beyond saying. When the early theologians of the church developed the doctrine of the incomprehensibility of God, this in fact is the main thing they had in mind. The eternal Father begets an eternal Son in an origination that does not take time. The *before* and *after* of time just do not apply, which means we barely know how to think or speak of it. This is why so much of our speaking about it has to be negative. We do not understand the eternal origin of the Son of God from the Father, but we know that there are things we cannot say, such as "there was once when he was not."

The earlier English translation of this phrase said the Son was begotten "before all worlds," which may be puzzling until we realize that one of the primary meanings of the English word "world" used to be "age."[12] So, for example, the old phrase "the next world" meant what the Bible calls the age to come, and "world without end" referred to the unending ages of the reign of Christ, whose kingdom has no end. We'll hear more about this later in the Creed.

The more recent translation, "eternally begotten," is a helpful paraphrase that tries to point to eternity as a realm beyond time, where things happen that don't have a beginning or end, or a *before* and *after*. It is as if the begetting of the Son of God were a timeless event, a way of coming into being that happened in a place without time or change or becoming—a place we are accustomed to call "eternity." Of course, we have no real familiarity with such a place and don't know how to conceive of it—we are dealing with incomprehensibility still. But this paradoxical picture of something we can't really picture can be helpful, as it suggests some of the right conceptual connections and negations: an eternal begetting is not a begetting in time; it has no *before* and *after*, no beginning or ending; it means there was never a time when the Father was without a Son; and so on.

Two final notes on terminology. First, the Latin translation of the Creed has a quirk at this point, as it renders the Greek word for "begotten" with a word meaning "born," so that the Latin Creed says, in effect, that the Son is "born of the Father." No difference in meaning from the Greek seems to be intended,[13] but to say that the Son is "born of" the Father does have a startling effect. It applies language to the Father that is ordinarily used of mothers. Of course, God the Father is not like any biological father, any more than he is like a biological mother. He is the sole source of the Son, not one of a pair of sexual beings reproducing themselves, as in pagan myths about the gods. But once you set aside clumsy literalism and false comparisons, the incomprehensibility of the doctrine here allows for a wide variety of language, all of which is inadequate but much of which is startlingly beautiful. For example, the Council of Toledo in AD 675 spoke of the Son being born "from the womb of the Father" (*de Patris utero*).[14] This strange statement is appropriate precisely because it pushes us beyond any father or mother we could ever imagine on earth, while acknowledging both as images of God (Genesis 1:27).

Second, it is worth knowing that many scholars use the label "eternal generation" for the eternal begetting of the Son of God. This reflects Latin vocabulary, in which the verb *generare* means "to beget." But of course the English word "generation" has a much broader meaning than "begetting," as it can refer to machines that generate electricity and ideas that generate debate. The deceptive familiarity of the word "generation" can therefore be misleading. Sticking with less familiar words like "begotten"—so long as the ordinary meaning of the word is understood—is more helpful both in guiding the imagination and in showing how far our imagination falls short of the reality.

[God from God]

The addition of this phrase is the trivial difference between the Latin and Greek versions of the Creed mentioned in the Introduction. This phrase is not in the original Greek version of the Nicene Creed, stemming from the Council of Constantinople in the year 381, but it is found in the earlier and shorter creed of the Council of Nicaea in 325 and was added to the Latin version. Hence most Western Christians find it familiar, while Eastern Orthodox Christians do not. Its meaning is repeated and reinforced in the subsequent phrase "true God from true God," so it presents no real disagreement between East and West—which is why the difference is, thank God, trivial.

In the Western versions of the Creed, this begins a series of three phrases that are meant to affirm, as plainly as possible, that Jesus is God. He is "God from God," which is to say, he is God the Son from God the Father. The Son derives his being from the Father, in such a way that he is just as fully God as God the Father is—as a human son is just as fully human as his father is. Unfortunately, these affirmations, while true, are not unambiguous. Something more will have to be said in the Creed to exclude misunderstandings, including the heretical notions of Arians who might say: "The Son is from God the same way every created thing is from God. He is not really God the same way the Father is. He is divine, but in a lesser sense. He is a secondary, intermediary deity."

The underlying problem here is that "God" is a very vague term. Its ancient equivalents, the Greek term *theos*, the Latin term *deus*, and even the Hebrew term *elohim*, could apply to any immortal being, including the angels and all the powers of heaven, which is why the LORD can be described in the Bible itself as a "great King above all gods" (Psalm 95:3). This is why Paul could say that there are indeed "many gods"

(1 Corinthians 8:5), before going on to affirm that "for us there is one God, the Father" (1 Corinthians 8:6). That is to say, Christians can acknowledge the existence of many immortal beings that are called gods or deities or divinities, but we worship only one God, the Father of our Lord Jesus Christ—so that when we bend the knee to Jesus as LORD, this is always "to the glory of God the Father" (Philippians 2:11). As we shall see later in the Creed, we glorify the Son and the Holy Spirit together in the same worship with which we worship God the Father. It is one worship because it is one God.

The problem is that this practice of Christian worship requires a conception of God that ancient Greeks and Romans did not have. They were used to gradations of divinity, from the supreme First Principle at the highest level, to a divine Mind (*Nous*) or Reason (*Logos*) serving as intermediary between the First Principle and the visible world, to the whole hierarchy of mythological deities, which could be taken literally or allegorically, depending on who you asked.

So to say that Jesus is God, in this ancient context, is not to say all that much. You could honor almost anyone as a "divine man" in the world of pagan antiquity, and Caesar (for example) was proclaimed as a god on Roman coins. If you really want to be clear about the nature of Jesus' divinity, you need to speak like a Jew, follow the New Testament, and confess that Jesus is LORD. But such a confession had no meaning outside the faith of Israel, so the Gentile believers of the fourth century needed a different terminology to make clear that they were not saying the kind of thing that pagans were saying about their gods. In the next few phrases of the Creed, we are working our way toward that strange new terminology, starting with terminology that is not quite so strange.

LIGHT FROM LIGHT

𝕿HIS SECOND ATTEMPT to say how the Son of God is divine is of course a metaphor, or we could call it an analogy (see the Excursus). Picking up the biblical metaphor that describes Jesus as "the radiance of the glory of God" (Hebrews 1:3), it pictures the light radiating from the sun as being of the same substance as the sun itself. This helps illustrate the key point that there was never a time when the Son of God did not exist, just as there was never a time when the sun was not shining. As the sun is never without the light that radiates from it, so God the Father is never without his Son.

The analogy is apt, but it also has definite limitations because it is comparing God to a material thing—as if God were made of some kind of stuff that is the same in the Son as in the Father. That of course cannot be literally true since, as we saw earlier, any stuff or material that exists belongs in the category of "all things" that are created by God; it results from his creative power and therefore cannot be in God from the beginning. So the Creator is not made up of any material, which is what is meant by describing him as an "immaterial being." Of course for some purposes we may find it helpful and illuminating to compare him to material things as Scripture does: water and rock, fire and shade, height and depth. But none of these comparisons can be taken literally. So once again for the purposes of the Nicene Creed, we have a phrase here that does not do enough to rule out misunderstandings and misinterpretations by the heretics.

TRUE GOD FROM TRUE GOD

𝕿HE TRANSLATION OF the Creed in older versions of the Book of Common Prayer and elsewhere uses the phrase "very God of very God," which can be confusing to people who don't know Latin. "Very," in this translation, is just an old word for "true" (from the Latin *verus*, "true," like the Latin *veritas*, "truth"). The word "of" can also be confusing; as it is used here and throughout the Creed (in the older translations) it means "from." It indicates origination, one thing coming from another.

Both the Father and the Son are designated "true God" in Scripture. John tells us in his first letter that the Son of God has come so that "we may know him who is true" and adds:

"We are in him who is true, in his Son Jesus Christ. He is the true God and eternal life" (1 John 5:20). And in the Gospel of John our Lord himself, praying to his Father, says his disciples have eternal life because "they know you, the only true God, and Jesus Christ whom you have sent" (John 17:3).

Yet once again, heretics can misunderstand. They can argue (and in the ancient world, they did argue) that because Jesus Christ is sent by the Father, he must be a servant who is less than the one who sent him. For once again, in pagan usage, "true God" might merely mean "truly divine," and that need not mean "equal to the supreme divine First Principle, the Father of all."

So the Creed will make one more attempt to clarify matters, introducing a crucial distinction.

Begotten, Not Made

MAKING AND BEGETTING are two fundamentally different ways to bring something into being. In the ordinary sense of the words, they designate the paradigmatic activities of art and nature, respectively. "Art" (Greek *techne*, Latin *ars*), in the original sense of these words that would have been familiar to the bishops at Nicaea and Constantinople, had a much broader meaning than it does now. It designated any kind of skill or craft. Anyone who made things well was practicing an art: carpenters and drill sergeants as well as sculptors and furniture makers. In just this sense, houses and armies and sculptures and furniture come into being by art, in contrast to the birds

73

and the bees, and horses and humans, which come into being by nature.

The first thing the Creed is saying when it contrasts begetting and making, therefore, is that the origination of the Son of God is more like something coming to be by nature than like something coming to be by art. The Creator of heaven and earth can be compared to an artist who makes all things well, by skill and wisdom. This is how "all things, visible and invisible" came to be. But it is not how the Son has his being from the Father. He is not one of the things God made; he is the natural-born Son of the Father, his only-begotten. Together with the Father and the Holy Spirit, he is, to use the technical term introduced in the discussion of the first article, "uncreated."

It turns out that the word "created," used in older translations ("begotten not created"), is also a technical term in theology. As Christian theology has traditionally used the term, creating is a unique kind of making, and only God can do it. Human beings make many things, but in the Bible and the traditional vocabulary of Christian theology, only God *creates*. Only God the Creator makes things out of nothing, needing no materials to work with. A human artist makes a pot out of clay or a house out of wood, but God is an artist who makes both pots and clay, houses and wood, and every element and particle that the clay and the wood are made out of. As Maker of all things, he cannot possibly have materials to work with except what he himself has made. He is the only Creator, the only Maker who makes things out of nothing. All things, visible and invisible, are his creation, and everything that has being, other than the Creator himself, is his creature. Every being is either creature or Creator, and there is no third category.

What the Creed is saying in this phrase is that the eternal Son of God does not belong in the category of "creature." He is not on the list of "all things" that God has made. As we saw in the first article of the Creed, he is not creature but Creator, just as truly as God the Father is. His role in the work of creation is different from the Father's, and we shall get to that shortly. And of course, when he becomes incarnate and is born of Mary, he does become a creature—and thus is the only being who is both creature and Creator in one. But right now the focus is on his being as Creator rather than creature, his divine nature rather than his human nature. With that focus in mind, we can extend our answer to the child's question: "Who created God?" The answer is that no one creates God. Not even God can create God. However, God can beget God—and he did.

The distinction between begetting and making or creating is a crucial clarification, but it too can only take us so far. Its import is mainly negative: the origination of the Son is not like the origination of something made by human or divine art. But negations have to be applied to begetting as well, for the Father eternally begetting the Son is not like any father on earth, nor is the begetting like the kind of thing that happens with earthly fathers or the genealogies in pagan mythology, where gods and goddesses become father and mother to new gods and goddesses. The Son is not a new or second God, and he has no mother except in his human nature, which is not the focus here. In his divine nature he comes directly from the Father, "from the being of the Father," as the earlier creed of the Council of Nicaea put it in 325. There cannot be any other source for the one whom we confess as "true God from true God."

But now we have just introduced the notion of "being," Greek *ousia*, which can also be translated "essence." This is a key component in the most difficult and unusual term in the Nicene Creed, to which we now turn.

Having the Same
Being as the Father

𝕿HIS PHRASE, ORIGINALLY introduced in the Creed of Nicaea in 325, contains the most famous, distinctive, and controversial word in the Nicene Creed of 381: *homoousios*, an unusual word even in Greek. It is composed of two ordinary Greek terms: the adjective *homo*, meaning "the same" (found in English words derived from Greek, such as "homogeneous" and "homonym"), and the noun *ousia*, a very broad word stemming from the Greek verb for "to be," which can mean "being" in any number of senses, such as an individual being, the fact that a thing exists, and the essence of something. "Essence" is a good rendering for the term as it is used in the Creed, narrowing down the possible meanings of *ousia* in a way that reflects how the term *homoousios* actually came to be used in Nicene theology. Using "one" rather than "the same" in translations of *homoousios* is not quite as helpful. Translations such as "of one being with the Father" and "of one essence with the Father" nicely reflect the insistence in Nicene theology that there is only one *ousia* or essence of God, but they do not suggest so forcefully the Nicene teaching that every divine attribute in the Son is *the same* as in the Father.[15]

The Council of Nicaea inserted the term *homoousios* into the Creed in order to exclude quite unmistakably the teachings of Arius and his followers, who could interpret (or rather misinterpret) other phrases in the Creed in a sense that was compatible with their heresy. But saying he had the same being or essence as the Father is something they could not accept. Although its precise meaning may have been unclear in the minds of many of the bishops at the Council, the fact that this phrase made the Son of God just as divine as the Father— divine in the same sense, not in a lesser sense—was evidently quite clear. This is why, over the years of controversy that followed the Council of Nicaea, the meaning of the word *ousia* headed in the direction of "essence." The Nicene teaching is that the Son has the same essence as the Father, in the sense that everything essentially divine is the same in God the Son as in God the Father: the Son has the same eternity, omnipresence, omnipotence, and omniscience as God the Father, and he is to be honored with the same worship.

Other translations of *homoousios* don't make this point as clear as it could be. Especially unfortunate are the translations, "of one substance with the Father" and "consubstantial with the Father." They both derive from the Latin word *substantia*, which is an old way of saying "essence." The problem is that the current meaning of "substance" in English refers usually to material of some kind or another, such as when we call salt or nitrous oxide a chemical substance, or when we speak of the substance used to make something. For example, we might say two rings are "of the same substance" if they are made out of the same material, such as gold. This material sense of "substance" is one possible meaning of the common Greek term *ousia*, but it is very clearly not the meaning the Council of Nicaea had in mind. Nicene theologians emphatically rejected the notion that the substance of God was material or that it could be divided, the way a lump of gold could be melted down and divided to make two or three rings. There is no such substance in God—there is no material out of which he is made—so when we speak of the *ousia* of the Father we must be referring to something quite different.

Anyone with a good grasp of Latin philosophical vocabulary will know that *substantia*, like *ousia*, does not have to mean *material* substance. But everyone else in a church that uses the word "consubstantial" or the phrase "of one substance with the Father" will nowadays find this language obscure at best and positively misleading at worst. For the sake of the vast majority of people saying the Creed in English, these are translations it would be better not to use.

Another possible meaning of *ousia* that can be eliminated from consideration is "individual being" (what the Nicene tradition later designates as *hypostasis*). If this were what the Council of Nicaea intended, then the Creed would be saying that the Son is the same being as the Father, as I might say that my son is the same being as the father of my grandchildren. If we interpreted *homoousios* in that way, then "Father" and "Son" would just be two names for the same thing. This is the heresy known as modalism or Sabellianism, and it is not the teaching of the Nicene faith.

Setting aside these misunderstandings, we are left with "being" as the nearest equivalent to the term *ousia*, and "essence" as the best one-word interpretation of the kind of being that Nicene teaching has in mind. The word "essence" itself, of course, has its ambiguities, but these actually help us understand the direction Nicene theology takes in subsequent centuries. To follow that direction, it is helpful to distinguish a modest and a strong sense of *homoousios*. The modest sense is what everyone who confesses the Nicene Creed is committed to: that the Son does not have a different kind of divine being from the Father. The strong sense is how you end up using the term when you carefully think through the consequences of applying it to God rather than to creatures: that every divine attribute in the Son is exactly the same thing as in the Father.

Nicene theology, by which I mean the thinking of the traditions that pledge allegiance to Nicaea, does in fact apply the term *homoousios* to creatures as well as the Creator. Most importantly, the Council of Chalcedon teaches that Jesus Christ is *homoousios* with us in his humanity, while he is *homoousios* with the Father in his divinity. The modest sense of "essence" captures the intent of the first half of this teaching. To say that he is *homoousios* with us human beings means that he has the same human essence as any human being, he shares human nature the way every human being does, and he has everything that is essential to being human (including, for example, both a human soul and a human body).

Applying that modest sense to the phrase "*homoousios* with the Father," we find that Chalcedon is interpreting the Nicene Creed to mean that the Son has every essential feature of divinity, and not some different kind of divinity than the Father. That is the sense of the term that excluded Arius' teaching, as well as every theology that subordinated the Son to the Father as if he were a secondary or lesser divine being. What this modest sense of *homoousios* does not do is explain how it is that Father and Son are one God. After all, that was not the purpose for which the Council of Nicaea inserted it into the Creed. But once you have the notion of a divine essence or *ousia* in your theology, you are going to have to ask what is unique about it—how it is different from the essence or *ousia* of any creature. That is what leads to the strong sense of *ousia* in Nicene theology.

The basic idea is that in God, everything is essential, which means it is unchangeable. For instance, the wisdom of God the Father is the same eternal and omniscient wisdom that belongs to God the Son. They are not even two examples of the same type of wisdom, like—say—the wisdom of Mary and the wisdom of John. For the wisdom of these two human beings changed as they grew and learned new things, and since neither of them was even close to omniscient, each one knew things the other didn't. All human wisdom is like that, full of details that others don't know, such as knowledge of our own hometown and family. But between God the Father and God the Son there is no such difference: they know exactly the same things and have exactly the same wisdom, for there is only one wisdom of God, which they both have. Hence the conclusion that follows from the strong sense of *homoousios*: as the divine essence is the same in the Father and in the Son—and in the Holy Spirit as well—there is in God only one wisdom, one knowledge, and likewise only one almighty power and one will, and furthermore only one eternity and one omnipresence.

A later confession in the Nicene tradition illustrates this point memorably, speaking of "the eternal Father, the eternal Son, and the eternal Holy Spirit—and yet not three Eternals, but one Eternal" and "likewise, the Father Almighty, the Son Almighty, and the Holy Spirit Almighty—and yet not three Almighties but one Almighty."[16] Hence in conclusion: "God the

Father, God the Son, and God the Holy Spirit, and yet there are not three Gods but one God." By the time the Nicene tradition gets to this point, *homoousios* has obviously been applied to the Holy Spirit as well as to the Son, so the Nicene teaching is that the *ousia* or essence of the Father is no different from that of the Son and of the Holy Spirit. It is the one essence of the one God, utterly the same in the Father, the Son, and the Holy Spirit. This is the strong sense of *homoousios*, which it is not necessary to know in order to confess the Nicene Creed, but to which Nicene theology inevitably leads when its logic is followed with care.

A few more notes on philosophical terminology may be helpful for those who wish to embark on further study. As the Nicene tradition develops, the term "nature" (*physis* in Greek, *natura* in Latin) comes to be used as an equivalent to *ousia* or essence. Hence, Jesus is *homoousios* with us because he shares human nature with us, and he is *homoousios* with the Father because the one divine nature belongs fully and equally to Father, Son, and Holy Spirit.

Another term that designates the divine nature is "Godhead," which is a very outdated piece of English that confuses many students. Nowadays if we were to make up a word like this, it would be something like "Godhood." Once you get used to it, however, it's a handy word for everything that is essential to or characteristic of God. You could also use the word "divinity," parallel to the way we use the word "humanity" to designate what all human beings have in common. But since "divinity" is a very vague term (as we have seen in pagan usage) some scholars still find it worthwhile to use the old term "Godhead," which is nowadays used only by Christians, to designate the one divine essence or *ousia*.

And one final note—about the beauty of the Nicene teaching. The phrase from the original Creed of Nicaea that says the Son was begotten "from the being of the Father" is worth thinking about. The divine *ousia*, the being or essence of God, belongs equally to Father, Son, and Holy Spirit; but it originates with the Father, who bestows it entirely on the Son when he gives the Son his very being, and likewise on the Spirit, whose very being originates from the being of the Father, who is the source of all divine being. It is a lovely thought: the Father becomes Father—becomes himself—by eternally giving all that is his to the Son, as the Son becomes himself by eternally receiving all that he is from the Father. This is the power of divine love, the one love of God in which the Holy Spirit too fully participates, receiving all that he is and has from the Father, who is the source of all that is divine.

Through Whom All
Things Came to Be

THE GREEK VOCABULARY here is entirely the same as in John 1:3, which describes the creation of the world through the Word which was with God in the beginning: "All things came to be through him, and without him not one thing came to be."[17] Once again, as in the first article, we are confronted with the contrast between "all things" and the Creator of all things. But here the verb (*egeneto*) is a very broad term for what comes to be or happens or becomes something. Often in older translations the verb is rendered "was made," mainly due to the influence of Latin, where the way to say that something came to be is to say it was made to be so (*factus est*). But it is useful to stick with the more precise rendering, "came to be," so as to be clear about the difference between this and the verb "to make" (*poein* in Greek).

John's use of this verb underlines that all things owe their coming into being to the Word of God. It gives us a different model of creation than the picture of an artist making things by the skill of his hands. It is more like "he commanded and they were created" (Psalm 148:5) and "God said, 'Let there be light,' and there was light" (Genesis 1:3). The two models are not in conflict, but both point to the unique and incomprehensible power of divine creation, which is not like the way any creature brings things into being. Things come to be by God's creation in a different way than when a builder constructs a house or an author writes a book or a musician composes a symphony. All of these things are human products that are also divine creations, for they are items on the list of "all things," and not one of them came into being without the Word of God. So the unique creativity of God is not in competition or conflict with the artistry of creatures who make things like houses and books and symphonies.

Theologians have helpfully distinguished between the "primary causality" of God as First Cause and Creator, and the entirely different and lesser power that is the "secondary causality" of creatures making things, such as builders and authors and composers. We can picture the difference as that between a chain of causes and effects operating horizontally on a timeline, and the vertical power that supports the whole timeline and maintains it in being, as God holds all creation and its history in his hand. The difference used to be easier to talk about, because until the eighteenth century people did not speak of human beings as "creative." The Bible and theology were well-known enough that only God was described as creating things. Nowadays, by contrast, we have to contend with the expanded usage of words like "create" and "creativity," which can make it seem that if an artist created a painting, God is not its Creator—which is false. The painting, like the artist herself, is on the list of "all things," not one of which came to be without the Word of God. This is a both/and proposition, as both primary and secondary causality—both vertical and horizontal power—are real. It is because God is the Creator of all things, bringing the whole timeline into being, that the artist is really and truly the maker of the painting. For by the Word of God all things really and truly come to be.

Excursus

The Word and Analogies

$\mathcal{T}$HE ONLY-BEGOTTEN SON of God is also called the Word (Greek *Logos*). So despite the fact that the term "Word" is not used in the Nicene Creed, it is an important term to know about if you want to understand the teaching of the Nicene church fathers. This excursus therefore provides a quick dive into Trinitarian terminology outside the Creed for those who wish to study further. For a simpler presentation of the doctrine of the Trinity, without the technical terms, see the Epilogue.

The connection between "Word" and "Son" is made by way of the term "only-begotten" (*monogenes*), as it is used in the prologue in the first chapter of the Gospel of John. On the one hand, the term is connected to the Son, because it looks forward to the wonderful passage in chapter three about God sending his only-begotten Son into the world to save the world (John 3:16). On the other hand, it also looks back to the very first words of the Gospel, about the Word who was with God in the beginning (John 1:1). For the term "only-begotten" first shows up in the great verse about the incarnation of the Word: "And the Word became flesh and dwelt among us, and we beheld his glory, glory as of the only-begotten of the Father" (John 1:14, NKJV).[18] In this great verse "the only-begotten" refers to the same person who is also described as "the Word." Drawing all the connections together, it is clear that the only-begotten Son *is* the Word that was in the beginning with God.

So the church fathers had good reason, when thinking of the beginning of all things, to refer first to the Word. The prologue of the Gospel of John is giving us what theologians call a *protology*, an account of beginnings, to match the *eschatology*, the account of the end and goal of all things, given in

Philippians 2:10–11, when every knee shall bow and every tongue confess that Jesus is LORD. If that glory reveals who Jesus is in the end, then what is he to begin with? John's answer is: he is the Word, the *Logos* that was in the beginning with God (John 1:1) and through whom all things came to be (John 1:3).

The term "Word" has a complex history, as it resonated deeply with the language of ancient philosophy, where *Logos* meant Reason as well as Word. The church fathers saw this and could not but think of the divine Reason by which the world was formed, identifying it with the Wisdom that was with the LORD at the beginning of his work of creation (Proverbs 8:22–31) and also with Christ as the Power of God and the Wisdom of God (1 Corinthians 1:24). One of the consequences of Nicaea, however, is that this divine Reason or *Logos* could not be conceived the way the philosophers thought of it, as a kind of subordinate, intermediary being between the divine First Principle above all things and the created world beneath, as if the *Logos* were a third kind of being, in the middle between God and the world, not fully God but not exactly part of the creation. The Nicene Creed recognizes no intermediary being between God and creation. Everything that exists is either the Creator or a creature, with no third kind of being. Therefore nothing mediates between God and the creation except the one who is both Creator and creature, the man Jesus, who is the "one mediator between God and men" (1 Timothy 2:5). As God incarnate, he is not a third kind of being but rather a both/ and—both Creator and creature—for he is both God and man in one person.

Once that point was clear, theologians could use the term "Word" in analogies that might help us understand how there is only one God, even though God is Father, Son, and Holy Spirit—or, we can now also say, God, Word, and Spirit. To build an analogy based on the latter three terms, you can think of the human word or *logos* as the inner rational thought or conception of a mind that also has will or love as the characteristic of its spirit. That gets you three different realities—mind, thought, and love—which remain distinct but do not add up to three human beings, just as God and his Word and his Spirit remain distinct but do not add up to three Gods. This kind of psychological analogy, as it has come to be called, has played an important role in Western theology, beginning especially with Augustine, the great African church father, and in medieval theologians such as Thomas Aquinas.

Excursus   97

But of course the analogy can only take us so far. Augustine insists on this, harping on the inadequacy and limitation of every analogy for God, because every analogy is based on some kind of likeness, and no likeness of God is equal to God except the Son of God himself. As one medieval church council put it (Lateran IV, in 1215): in every likeness to God there is a greater unlikeness. There is no paradox in this, since any two things that are alike in one respect are also unlike in other respects. What is distinctive is that the unlikeness to God is always greater than the likeness. Thomas Aquinas helps explain this by pointing out that any likeness to God is asymmetrical. Creatures can be like God, as Genesis 1:26 says, but the reverse is not true: God is not like anything in creation.[19] Likeness is, as it were, hierarchical: the lower can be like the higher, but the higher is not like the lower—just as your image in a mirror is your likeness, but you are not its likeness. It resembles you, but you don't resemble it.

Because every analogy or likeness of God is limited and imperfect, each needs to be supplemented by other analogies or likenesses. Hence the psychological analogies, rooted in the biblical vocabulary of God and his Word, cannot be used without the social analogies suggested by the biblical vocabulary of Father and Son. The latter is the vocabulary of the Creed because it is the vocabulary of Christian baptism in the name of the Father, and of the Son, and of the Holy Spirit. It is also the basis for an important set of technical terms in Trinitarian theology, according to which there are three persons in God, or three *hypostases* having one essence or *ousia*. There shall be important clarifications to make about this technical terminology when we come to speak of the Holy Spirit.

BELIEVE IN ONE GOD, TH
OF HEAVEN AND EARTH, O
NVISIBLE. I BELIEVE IN O
ONLY BEGOTTEN SON OF
BEFORE ALL AGES. GOD FR
TRUE GOD FROM TRUE G
CONSUBSTANTIAL WITH
ALL THINGS WERE MADE
SALVATION HE CAME DOW
HOLY SPIRIT WAS INCARNA
BECAME MAN. FOR OUR SA
PONTIUS PILATE, HE SUFFI
AND ROSE AGAIN ON THE
WITH THE SCRIPTURES. HE
S SEATED AT THE RIGHT H
COME AGAIN IN GLORY TO
DEAD AND HIS KINGDOM W
N THE HOLY SPIRIT, THE LO
PROCEEDS FROM THE FATH
THE FATHER AND THE SON
WHO HAS SPOKEN THROUG
IN ONE, HOLY, CATHOLIC
CONFESS ONE BAPTISM
SINS AND I LOOK FORWAR
THE DEAD AND THE LIFE O

ARTICLE 2, PART 2

GOD INCARNATE

WHO FOR US HUMAN BEINGS
AND FOR OUR SALVATION

𝕳 ERE FOR THE first time the Creed turns to us, to the human race. Yet it is still telling God's story, not ours. The story is the good news of who God is and what he has done for us in Christ. We are in this story as those on the receiving end of what God does for our salvation. So the Creed does not give us anything to do, like the law and its commandments. It does not tell us how to get saved, but instead confesses faith in Christ the savior, God incarnate. This is why Martin Luther regards the Creed as a summary of the gospel, the saving word of God that gives us Christ—and in him gives us salvation—to be received by faith alone.

The gospel story is for the whole world, including the whole of humanity. The ancient versions of the Creed are quite clear on this point, using the generic terms for human beings in Greek and Latin (*anthropous* and *homines*) rather than the terms for human males. Unfortunately the English language tried to get by for centuries using "men" for both. My translation above reflects the usage of the original languages.

One further grammatical point before we proceed. The Creed down to the middle of the third article is one long sentence in Greek. The second article, until its last phrase, consists entirely of a series of verb phrases with the same grammatical subject: "One Lord, Jesus Christ, the only-begotten Son of God." This subject is modified by two "who" clauses, beginning with "who was begotten from the Father before all ages" and "who for us human beings and for our salvation came down from heaven." As we shall see, it is a matter of great importance that all the verbs in these clauses have one and the same grammatical subject.

Came Down from Heaven

$\mathfrak{F}$ROM THE PERSPECTIVE of the Creed, the most important thing about heaven is that Jesus is there at the right hand of the Father. This again is the heaven of heavens, the place beyond places of which there will be more to say when the Creed comes to speak of his ascension. What the present phrase tells us is that before he ascended, he descended. "No one has ascended into heaven except he who descended from heaven" (John 3:13). He came to us from heaven, where the angels have already been worshiping him in glory from the beginning. He comes from there, but he was not content to remain there. Love brought him down, so that he might dwell among us and we might behold his glory, the glory of the only-begotten of the Father (John 1:14).

This is characteristic of heaven, which throughout the Bible is described in terms of what it gives to the earth. It begins in the first chapter of Genesis with the creatures in the visible heaven that give light to the earth: the sun and moon making times and seasons, years, months, and days from their movements above us (Genesis 1:14–15). From the visible heaven comes also the power of life for all things on earth, with rain watering the fields and the sun bestowing its warmth and energy upon everything that grows up from the ground. Hence David can compare a good king to the sun shining on a cloudless morning and the rain that makes grass spring up from the earth (2 Samuel 23:2). For every good and perfect gift comes from above, from the Father of lights (James 1:17), who dwells in light inaccessible (1 Timothy 6:16) above all the luminaries and movements of the visible heaven, in a realm where nothing grows old and dies. Yet the light of heaven keeps descending to bestow its life-giving energy upon the ever-changing earth, where life can only be flesh, going through birth and growth and decay and death.

When we pray for the coming of the kingdom of God, we are asking for what heaven alone can give the earth: that our Father's good will, his heavenly justice and mercy and steadfast love, may rule "on earth as it is in heaven" (Matthew 6:10). Like farmers waiting for sun and rain, we await gifts from above, including the light of revelation. From the invisible realm of God's throne above, hidden from our eyes and minds, good things are prepared to be revealed and to shine forth at the right time. Thus at the time when Israel was brought out of Egypt, the pattern of the tabernacle was revealed to Moses on the mountain, so that worship on earth might begin to imitate worship in the heavenly temple that is not made with hands (Hebrews 8:5). So also Paul speaks of the mystery of Christ "hidden for ages in God, who created all things" (Ephesians 3:9), which has now been revealed by the Spirit through the prophets and apostles (Ephesians 3:5): the mystery which is, quite simply, Jesus Christ (Colossians 1:27, 2:2).

The coming of Christ from heaven is the new revelation of what is older than the foundation of the earth. Unlike rain and sunshine coming down from the visible heavens, it does not require a physical movement from one place to another. This is the descent of the Creator himself, who is by nature present in everything he has made. All of creation is held in his hand, and there can be no distance in space between him and any creature. Thus Augustine explains his descent: "He is said to have come to us, not from place to place through space, but by appearing to mortals in mortal flesh. He came to a place where he was already."[20] The Creator cannot possibly be absent from any place he created—even when we go down to the place of the dead, he is there (Psalm 139:8)—but what he can do is reveal himself in an utterly new way, making manifest his grace prepared in heaven from the beginning, the mystery of salvation that has been hidden for long ages but now is revealed in human flesh, which has in Jesus Christ become God's own flesh. This is the descent of the only-begotten Son of God that the Creed now follows.

And Was Incarnate

"**I**NCARNATION" IS THE name for the Christian doctrine about who Jesus is, with a focus on his being both God and man. He is the only-begotten Son of God who has become one of us, as fully human as he is fully God. The Greek term the Creed uses here for his humanity, *sarkothenta*, refers to flesh and could be translated, if we wanted to be hyper-literal, as "was fleshified." It is based on the noun *sarx*, from which we get "sarcophagus," the place to bury dead flesh. The word suggests mortality and weakness, things that can suffer and die. The Latin term, *incarnatus*, reflected here in the English, is based on the root word *carnem*, which like the Spanish word *carne* and the English word "flesh" can refer to the meat of an animal such as beef or pork in chili con carne. This is another side of his coming down from heaven: it is a real come-down for God to become a piece of meat, just like we are, an animal who is born and eats and defecates and dies, the kind of creature who could quite literally become a meal for a carnivore.

God *chooses* this. This choice is what the Bible indicates when it says he "humbled himself" (Philippians 2:8). To be humbled is to be humiliated, lowered, put in a lowly place, like someone required to sit at the back of the bus or far from the head of the table (Luke 14:9). No other human being chose to be what all of us are: animals who are born and suffer and die. God alone could *choose* to be human—and did. This is his eternal "election," to use the theological term derived from the Latin word for "choice." The grace of this election, the love of God by which he chose to be human, is the secret at the heart of human history and the whole universe of creation; it is the mystery hidden from the beginning and now made known, preached by the apostles, written in the Scriptures, and taught by the Creed.

The term "incarnation" has had a long history since the Creed, and is no longer used only by Christians. So we need to be clear: when the Creed uses the term, it is referring to no one but Jesus Christ. Incarnation is not the same as embodiment, for every living human being is embodied, but only Christ is God incarnate. Nor should it be confused with reincarnation, a modern term for an ancient religious doctrine that is alien to Christianity. Reincarnation is a very widespread notion, common in ancient Greece as well as India, that is almost always tied to the desire to escape from embodiment and the wheel of rebirth by which each soul keeps coming to earth as yet another human being who suffers and dies. It is a desire pushing people in the opposite direction from the humiliation that the Son of God chose for himself in becoming flesh.

The Hebrew term for "flesh" in Scripture refers to everything about a human being that is vulnerable and needy, subject to hurt, trauma, wounds, and disease.[21] It was translated into Greek by the word *sarx*, pointing to death and decay as the key characteristics of our bodies, the thing we are that goes into the ground and rots. Paul speaks of the undoing of death and decay when he says of the body that is laid to rest in Christ: "This corruptible must put on incorruption, and this mortal must put on immortality" (1 Corinthians 15:53, NKJV). The Greek term for "corruption" is the ugly word *phthora*—you can hardly say it without spitting—which can refer to anything that decays and goes bad. Corruptibility, the tendency to decay, is the way of all flesh, and its end is death. What the Son of God has done by taking on our flesh reverses our corruptibility, clothing all our mortal weakness with the glorious power of everlasting life. For his flesh is the flesh of God himself, given for the life of the world, so that in the body of Christ we have the wonder of life-giving flesh (John 6:51).

As a final note, translations that say he "*became* incarnate" are adding something that the Creed avoids saying. The notion of becoming (or coming to be) belongs in the world of changing things, things that come to be and also cease to be. The church fathers, convinced that God is unchanging, avoided speaking this way of God, even when describing the incarnation. We will see more about how they managed to avoid this when we get to the phrase rendered in English as "became human."

FROM THE HOLY SPIRIT

T HE ELECTION OF God, the choice of the only-begotten Son to humble himself and take on our flesh, is carried out by the Holy Spirit, who is mentioned now for the first time in the Creed. For he is the Life-Giver, and this is the central moment in which God gives life to his creation. He is the one who speaks through the prophets, and this is the great revelation of God on earth to which the prophets bear witness. He is the one who completes and brings to perfection every work of God, and thus he shall be with the church, the Body of Christ, throughout its life in the world and in the age to come.

We have here the Creed's most important statement about what the church's tradition calls "the Trinity." Every work of God is the one work of the Father, the Son, and the Holy Spirit. Like the very essence of God, it originates with the Father, is given to the Son, and is brought to completion by the Holy Spirit. Thus the Greek church father Gregory of Nyssa says that God's power always "flows forth from the Father as from a spring, is put to work by the Son, and the grace is perfected by the power of the Holy Spirit."[22] The fact that every work of God is the work of the Father, the Son, and the Holy Spirit in one action is fundamental for Gregory, because it is why Christians insist that there is only one God. The oneness of God's work is not mere cooperation, as Paul and Barnabas and Silas might work together in the same ministry—and then perhaps have a falling out and go their separate ways. There is only one God, so every work of God is necessarily and inseparably the work of the whole Trinity: Father, Son, and Holy Spirit.

But the work of incarnation is not done by the Trinity alone, for there is human participation in it from the time it begins on earth. The original Greek of the Nicene Creed simply joins this human contribution to the divine work by speaking of the Holy Spirit and the Virgin Mary together as objects of the preposition "from" (*ek*). The standard Latin translation, reflected in many English versions, hints at the difference between them by speaking of Christ being incarnate "of" (*de*) the Holy Spirit and "from" (*ex*) the Virgin Mary. And some recent translations add a paraphrase to make the difference explicit: "By the power of the Holy Spirit." This phrasing picks up on the biblical passage that is the basis for this part of the Creed, where the angel announces to Mary that the Holy Spirit shall come upon her as "the power of the Most High" over-shadowing her (Luke 1:35). For the power that makes the incarnation of God possible is God's power alone, the one power of the Trinity: Father, Son, and Holy Spirit. Yet it would not be the full grace of the incarnation without a human partner, to whom the Creed now turns.

AND THE VIRGIN MARY

T HE ACTUAL WORD order, in both the Greek and the Latin, is "Mary the Virgin." It is worth bearing in mind that her name comes first, then her condition. Over the centuries the description of her condition has become so firmly attached to her name that it has in effect become part of it, as "Christ" has become attached to the name of Jesus and has given us the name "Jesus Christ." She is named by most Christians, especially Roman Catholics, as the Blessed Virgin Mary. "Blessed," too, has become as if part of her name, as she herself sings in her beautiful astonishment: "All generations will call me blessed" (Luke 1:48).

She sings, magnifying the name of the LORD, because he has done great things with her (Luke 1:49). By the power of the Holy Spirit, with no help from a man—that is the crucial significance of her virginity—he has made her, as her cousin Elizabeth bears witness, "the mother of my Lord" (Luke 1:43). The Latin tradition therefore calls her Mother of God (*Mater Dei*) and the Greek tradition, "God-bearer" (*Theotokos*). She bears God in that she bears and gives birth to Jesus, who is true God from true God. And she is the Mother of God in that she is the mother of the true God, Jesus; she is the human being from whom he took human flesh, like any baby growing within his mother and being nourished by her lifeblood. For he is as truly human as any child in the womb and as truly God as God the Father.

To say that Mary is the Mother of God therefore does not mean something preposterous like saying she is the origin of God. The Creed has already made abundantly clear the divine origin of Jesus Christ: he is the only-begotten Son of the Father before all ages. So the church fathers teach that there are two births of the Son of God, a birth in eternity and a birth in time. He is eternally begotten of the Father before all worlds and times, and also is born of the Virgin Mary at a particular time and place in this world. His divinity begins with God the Father, but his humanity begins with the work of the Holy Spirit in the obedience of Mary the Virgin.

Her obedience is summed up beautifully in the Latin tradition by the word *fiat*, from the phrase *fiat mihi secundum verbum tuum*, "let it be to me according to your word" (Luke 1:38), which follows her humble self-description, *ecce ancilla Domini*, "behold, the handmaid of the LORD" (Luke 1:38, KJV). She is submitting in humility, like a willing slavegirl—for that is what the term politely translated "handmaiden" actually means. Like the humiliation of the Son of God who takes on the form of a slave in Philippians 2:7 (politely translated "servant"), this is real humility—indeed humiliation—not the posturing of someone claiming to be humble. As she later sings, after her cousin has spoken of her greatness, "he has looked upon the lowliness of his slavegirl" (Luke 1:48).[23] She is not talking about her virtues but about her littleness, her low place in the scheme of things, which the LORD has now utterly overturned so that he too may be humbled and lowly with her.

Her *fiat*, "let it be," is the same as the first word God speaks in the Latin Bible when he says in the beginning, *fiat lux*, "let there be light" (Genesis 1:3). Because of God's *fiat* there is creation, the existence of all things, whereas because of Mary's *fiat* there is redemption, the man Jesus, who is God making all things new. Her merely human obedience is the lowliness through which the eternal Son of God comes down from heaven. Her humble *fiat*, echoing the word of power by which all things came to be, is the greatest purely human contribution to the salvation of the world. Rightly do all generations call her blessed.

We see about as far into the depth of divine humility as possible when we notice that the Creed is saying: the one who is born of Mary the Virgin is the same one who is eternally begotten of the Father. The Nicene Creed says this in the most direct possible way by having one and the same grammatical subject for all the verbs in the second article of the Creed up to this point. The verb "begotten" has the same grammatical subject as the verb "became incarnate," which has the same subject as the verbs "became human" and "was crucified." The statement of faith by the ecumenical Council of Chalcedon in 451 drives home this point by using the phrase "the same one" five times in one long sentence describing "one and the same Son, who is our Lord Jesus Christ." The result is so repetitive that few English translations actually include every instance of "the same one," because it makes for such an awkward sentence. But it is best to keep it in, so as to hit ourselves over the head with what is, in effect, the Chalcedonian interpretation of the Nicene Creed. The same one who is eternally begotten of the Father is the same one who came down from heaven, the same one who was incarnate of the Holy Spirit and Mary the Virgin, the same one who was crucified under Pontius Pilate, the same one who thus suffered and was buried, the same one who rose again and is enthroned now at the right hand of the Father.

Using the same grammatical subject for all these verbs is the way the Creed describes the one who is both the second person of the Trinity and the man Jesus. The term "person" here has an ancient technical meaning in theology, as we shall see when discussing the Holy Spirit, the third person of the Trinity, but the point of its use is captured in a less technical way by the simple grammar of the Creed. What Christian theology means by saying Jesus is one person with two natures is presented in the Creed when it speaks of the same one— the same grammatical subject—having two births, as he is both begotten of the Father and also born of the Virgin Mary. Because he has these two births, he is both truly God and truly human.

And Became Human

ONCE AGAIN, AS in the phrase "through whom all things came to be," the Latin says "was made" (*factus est*) rather than "came to be" or "became," and older English translations follow suit, saying he "was made man." The Greek, however, avoids the language of making and becoming. To translate hyper-literally again, the Son of God was not only "fleshified" but "in-humanized." The Creed thus avoids suggesting that he *becomes* something different or *is made* something else when he is incarnate. Rather, as the Greek church father Gregory Naziansen puts it, "he remained what he was and took up what he was not."[24] That is to say, he remains unchanged as the eternal Son of God even as he assumes our suffering and mortal humanity and makes it his own.

For the Son of God to take up our flesh is for him to be fully human. And in the Bible, as we have seen, flesh means the whole of human nature in its vulnerability, corruptibility, and need. So "flesh" is not just "body." The soul, the mind, and the heart can be wounded, traumatized, diseased, and corrupted. There is no part of us that is invulnerable to sin and suffering. So if God is to save our souls as well as our bodies, he must make the human soul his own, including the human mind and reason and will. For as Gregory Naziansen also mentioned, what is not taken up and assumed is not healed.[25]

The verb for "assumed" or "taken up" reflects the language of Philippians 2:7, where Christ in the form of God "took upon him the form of a servant" (KJV). The church fathers use this verb frequently to make the point that the Son of God did not become man by becoming other than God. He did not cease to be the eternal God but assumed our humanity, taking up a human soul and body and making it his own. He did not become less than God but added our vulnerable humanity to his unchanging divinity, thus joining humanity and divinity in one person.

This is what the Council of Chalcedon had in mind when it taught that Jesus is "true God and true man." His humanity does not make him less than God, and his divinity does not make him other than human. He is not just God looking human, like an angel who might temporarily appear in human form. If you read much of the church fathers, you will find them saying that he is "perfect man," which is not a reference to his moral perfection—there are other words for that—but to his being completely human, as fully human as we are, having body and soul and mind and all that belongs to human nature.

He is without sin, of course, but sin does not belong properly to human nature. It is how human nature gets corrupted, bent and twisted out of its natural shape. By his sinlessness, Jesus lives in the full integrity of human life intended by God from the beginning, untainted by the foul deformity of sin. He initiates the restoration of human nature by being perfectly human, without spot or blemish, like a lamb ready for the Passover sacrifice (Exodus 12:5). Biblical sacrifice always requires spotlessness, an animal that is uninjured and undamaged, perfect in its kind (Leviticus 1:3, 3:1, 4:3, etc.). Hence in the great sacrifice to end all sacrifices, we have one who is not literally a lamb but a perfect man, unblemished, acceptable and well-pleasing to God, offered up for us (Hebrews 9:14).

And Was Crucified Also for Us under Pontius Pilate

T HE CREED TOUCHES only so briefly on the cross of Christ, his sacrifice and atonement. The most important thing it has to say about it is that the crucifixion of the Son of God is not something that just happened to take place. Rather, it is *for us*, which means it belongs to the whole sequence of what the Creed says God has done *for us human beings and our salvation.* Through Pontius Pilate, of all people, God's will is done on earth as in heaven. Carrying out his eternal plan, God in the fullness of time handed over his Son for us (Romans 8:32), which meant that Pilate handed him over to be crucified

(Matthew 27:26, John 19:16) after Judas handed him over to his enemies (Matthew 26:16, 26:46). In Greek it's all the same verb—translated "handed over" or "delivered" or, sometimes, "gave him up"—showing how human beings, whether they know it or not, keep doing things that fulfill God's purpose of salvation. In his sovereign providence, God does what he does through what we do.

So God has a use for people like Pilate, who serve his purposes whether they know it or not. This accords with God's providence, which is the triumphant power of God's love for us. The gospel of Jesus Christ is the story of the whole world and its history; it is *God's* story, and nothing we do gets us out of it. We may be humbly obedient like Mary or cruelly unjust like Pilate, but always God's will shall be done through us and our deeds. And his will is what he does in love for us and for our salvation.

Of course, the really hard part in what God does is the burden borne by God himself in his own flesh. The logic of the second article of the Creed, with its sequence of verbs all having the same grammatical subject, has the consequence that we can rightly say it is God who hangs on the cross for us. For the same one who is true God from true God is the same one who was born of Mary the Virgin and is also the same one who was crucified under Pontius Pilate. So the logic of the flesh in Mary's womb applies also to the flesh on Pilate's cross. Just as she is the Mother of God because the baby she bears is true God from true God, so the cross that bears Jesus bears the true God, the one who is rightly called by the name of the LORD. Yet just as Mary does not originate Jesus' divine nature, which is his because he is begotten of the Father before all ages, so the cross does not destroy his divine nature, which is eternal and unchanging and remains immortal even as he dies, thereby defeating death as only the immortal God can do.

And Suffered

WHAT GOD DOES to save us is what is done to his Son. This is only one of the paradoxes built into this word, "suffered"—*pathonta* in Greek and *passus* in Latin, words that signify pathos and passivity, not activity. This is why we call the events of the crucifixion Christ's *passion*, not his action. In contrast to modern usage, which sees in "passion" a kind of energy and power, the ancient world used these words to refer not to what a person does but to what is done to him or happens in him, including passionate emotions that take control of a person's life without his being able to do anything about it. That is the sense inherent in the old contrast in English between "doing" and "suffering," which corresponds to the contrast between action and passion, or activity and passivity.

We need to grasp this sense of passion as suffering and passivity in order to get the paradox of God's working in Christ, which turns his human passion into a divine action—the working or energy of the Son of God doing his great deed of redeeming the world, which he does by suffering the horrible and shameful things done to him. Yet so far we have a relatively superficial paradox. Many a courageous person has done great things by suffering great wrongs. Our Lord goes to his suffering on the cross with courage born of love and obedience, which is wondrous but not a deep logical paradox.

The deep paradox, which the church fathers insisted on, stems from the truth that nothing can be done to God. He cannot be passive or suffer, for the divine nature and essence is to be active, creative, accomplishing all things, always cause and never effect. And yet there is the great both/and of incarnation: remaining what he was, he took up what he was not. He remained immortal, yet in the mortal flesh that he took up and made his own, he died. He remained impassible, which is to say beyond passion and suffering, yet he truly suffered in his passion. He suffered impassibly, as the church father Cyril of Alexandria put it, in an impassible passion.[26]

The paradox stems from the both/and of incarnation at the heart of the gospel story. The impassible suffers passion because God becomes man, Creator becomes creature, Word becomes flesh. The Creed presents this to us in the series of verbs in the second article, identifying the same one, the same grammatical subject, in his two births: begotten of the Father before all ages and yet born of Mary during the reign of Augustus Caesar—and the same one then crucified under Pontius Pilate some thirty years later, suffering and dying. When we set his suffering in the overarching narrative supplied by the verbs of the Creed, an interpretation of the paradox of the impassible passion suggests itself. It has in fact already been suggested above, in the discussion of his taking on flesh. For Jesus Christ alone, of all those who have ever suffered in the flesh, actively chose to make this passible flesh his own. Only God has the freedom to choose from the beginning to be human, to be mortal, to be born and suffer and die—and thus to make it his own action. In that sense, the impassible Son of God suffered more truly than any other human being, for only he suffers fully by his own act—not because suffering is imposed on him, but because in the power of divine love he has chosen to make a life of human suffering his very own life.

The original wording of the Nicene Creed, unlike the Apostles' Creed, does not explicitly mention Christ's death, but it is certainly not evading the fact that he died, as the next phrase makes clear. So the newer translations are not adding anything substantial by saying that "he suffered *death*." If anything, they are narrowing the vision of the Creed by focusing on the endpoint of his suffering rather than the whole lifetime our Lord Jesus spent suffering with us the effects of the wrath of God in this sinful world.

And Was Buried

The descent of the eternal Son of God to us mortals is completed here, as he travels the way of all flesh to the end, which is to be a corpse. In his burial our Lord joins the dead in their place under the earth, which the wrath of God allots them. He joins us under the judgment of God announced to Adam himself after his disobedience, telling him that he shall return to the ground, "for out of it you were taken; for you are dust, and to dust you shall return" (Genesis 3:19). Death is the endpoint of suffering and passion, in that we are never more passive than when we're dead. A corpse cannot do anything, but only have things done to it. Even its rotting and turning into dust is a process of corruption that happens in it, not a deed that it does. So it was with the only-begotten Son of God in the three days when he was none other than the dead man Jesus. His corpse was the flesh of the immortal God.

The Christian tradition goes further, accepting the common ancient definition of death put into circulation by Plato, who writes of Socrates on the day of his execution saying death is nothing other than the separation of the soul from the body.[27] If Socrates is right, then the eternal Son of God in his human death was united to both his soul and his body even in their separation. As the Eastern Orthodox liturgies put it most eloquently, in his body he has a Sabbath rest after his mighty work on the cross, while in his soul he goes down to the place of the dead, where he alone is "free among the dead."[28] He goes to the realm of the dead as the conqueror of death rather than its victim. For in the work of redemption that the tradition calls "the harrowing of hell," he frees all who were in the bosom of Abraham in the underworld awaiting his coming, and opens the kingdom of heaven to all believers.

The Creed does not go so far. It touches only so briefly on the three days when God is a dead man. But it commits us to confessing that it is so: that this same one who is the Son of

God begotten of the Father before all the ages, true God from true God, was crucified for us under Pontius Pilate, and that he himself—this same one—was buried like any other dead man.

And Rose Again on the Third Day according to the Scriptures

CHRISTIAN FAITH BEGINS here, with the confession that Jesus is the Lord and the faith that God raised him from the dead (Romans 10:9). He rose again, reversing his descent into the depths of death, and this rising again is what is meant by the Christian term, "resurrection of the dead." The Apostles' Creed, that other great creed of the church, calls it literally "the resurrection of the flesh." It is an event quite different from the widespread belief in the immortality of the soul (represented by Plato's *Phaedo*, for example), according to which the soul in us does not die. The resurrection is not about a part of us that doesn't die, but about God giving life to what is dead. Instead of a spark of immortality within us, the apostle pictures what is mortal in us being clothed with immortality (1 Corinthians 15:53). The difference is illustrated by the word of the angels at Jesus' tomb. They did not say, "His body is here, but his soul went to heaven," but rather, "He is not here, for he has risen" (Matthew 28:6). *He* is not there because his *body* is not in the tomb anymore. He is once again a living human being, and living human beings have living bodies that do not belong in the grave. For the resurrection of the dead is not just life after death; it is death itself being undone.

Not only Jesus' dying for our sins but also his burial and being raised on the third day took place "according to the Scriptures," says the apostle (1 Corinthians 15:3–4). When the New Testament says "Scriptures," it typically has the Old Testament in view. The Old Testament Scriptures, for example, give us the sign of Jonah, who was in the belly of the beast for three days and three nights (Jonah 1:17); so it is that the Son of Man will be "three days and three nights in the heart of the earth," says the Lord (Matthew 12:40). Christ sleeps for three days in "the dust of the ground" (Daniel 12:2, NASB), along with Adam, the "man of dust" (1 Corinthians 15:47; see Genesis 3:19) whose name reminds us of the Hebrew word for "ground" (*adamah*).

The apostle Peter, in his sermon on the day of Pentecost, quotes from the Scriptures a psalm of David and tells us that, being a prophet, David "foresaw and spoke about the resurrection of the Messiah, that he was not abandoned to the underworld, nor did his flesh see corruption" (Acts 2:31; see Psalm 16:10).[29] The word "underworld" here is *Hades* in Greek, representing *Sheol* in Hebrew—the place where the dead sleep in what the Scriptures call "the dust of the ground" and our Lord calls "the heart of the earth." The Apostles' Creed likewise says he descended to the underworld.[30] But he did not remain long with the dead in the underworld, Peter is saying, for "his flesh did not see corruption." That is to say, quite bluntly, that his body did not have time to decompose before his resurrection on the third day. That is how down-to-earth the news of his resurrection is.

AND ASCENDED INTO HEAVEN

THE ASCENSION IS not the same thing as the resurrection but is its continuation. As Christ in his flesh descended first into the Virgin's womb and thence to the place of the dead in the underworld, so now he first rises up from the dead and thence ascends all the way to highest heaven by the power of the life-giving Spirit of God. He is the Son of Man who comes on the clouds of heaven to the throne of the Ancient of Days, whose kingdom has no end (Daniel 7:13–14). As a cloud took him from our sight, so shall he return in "the same way," we are told (Acts 1:11)—which is to say in his living flesh, on a cloud that signifies "his glory and the glory of the Father and of the holy angels" (Luke 9:26).

Again, like his descent, this is not a movement from one place to another, for the heaven to which he ascends is the place beyond all places, the heaven above the visible heavens that we sing about in Psalm 148:4 ("Praise him, you highest heavens!") and that Solomon speaks of in his great prayer dedicating the temple: "The heaven and the heaven of heavens cannot contain thee" (1 Kings 8:27, KJV). It is the invisible dimension in which God, who is beyond all creation and yet never far from us—for no creature can ever be separated from him by spatial distance—is most intensely present to his creatures. It is not a location in physical space like the visible heavens (it would be absurd to try to travel there in a spaceship) but rather the dimension of the created world in which creatures are fulfilled in worship and contemplation of God, joining the angels who glorify him and enjoy him forever. It is the "place" of the King of kings, the sovereign power over every power, signified by the supreme height of the throne of God above all things, where he is "seated on high" and "looks far down on the heavens and the earth" (Psalm 113:5–6). This is the invisible heaven that may reveal itself at any place where

God is present in his glory and power and love, which is to say, at any place in creation.

Yet God is most intensely present, as Solomon's prayer says, in the particular places to which his attention turns when we call upon his Name. His eyes are open day and night to the place of which he says: "My Name shall be there" (1 Kings 8:29). Thus heaven's worship was imitated on earth at the tabernacle built according to the instructions revealed on Mt. Sinai to Moses, which in turn provided the pattern of the temple that Solomon built in Jerusalem, the holy place in the holy city under the rule of the Son of David. This is the place God chooses as the dwelling place of his Name (Deuteronomy 16:2), the place where his eyes turn and his ears are especially open to the prayers of his people (1 Kings 8:30–40). The temple in Jerusalem is thus the precursor of the everlasting temple which is Christ's own resurrected body, the enduring place of God's most intensive presence, in whom dwells the Name of him who is King of kings and Lord of lords, who sits on the everlasting throne above all things and ever lives to make intercession for us before the Father (Hebrews 7:25).

And Sits at the Right Hand of the Father

Up to this point, the Creed has been summarizing the story of the gospel of Jesus Christ; with his arrival at the right hand of the Father, the story comes to the present. We live on earth today under Christ in heaven—the crucified man who was once dead and buried but now lives forever at God's right hand, which means that infinite power is his, always and everywhere, above all things. We have reached what is, narratively, the center point of the Creed, which pivots now from the story of how Christ came to be in the world to the story of what he is doing to rule and redeem it and, by his Spirit, to bring about a future of life everlasting.

"Sits" here means "is enthroned." The Creed is inviting us to picture the man Jesus sharing the throne of God. The picture stems from a Scripture passage often quoted in the New Testament: "The LORD says to my Lord: 'Sit at my right hand, until I make your enemies your footstool' " (Psalm 110:1). As we have seen in discussing the phrase, "one God," the English term "the LORD," written with four capital letters, represents the sacred and unutterable Name of the God of Israel, while "Lord" with only one capital letter is the ordinary Hebrew word for "Lord." What is of particular interest in this psalm is the relation of the one term to the other. Like Psalm 2 (discussed in connection with "the only-begotten Son of God"), Psalm 110 seems originally to have envisioned the enthronement of the son of David, the king who is the adopted son of God. But Jesus shows us that it ultimately points beyond that (Mark 12:35–37). Since this is a psalm of David, what we hear in this passage is David the king honoring the Son of David as his Lord, enthroned at the right hand of the LORD. Our Lord Jesus asks us to consider: How could David be calling his own son or descendant "my Lord"? The Creed provides the answer Christian faith gives to that question: Christian faith. The ultimate Son of David, the Anointed One whose kingdom has no end, is the only-begotten Son of God, our Lord Jesus who descends from David and comes in the name of the LORD, to whom is given this Name that is above every name (Philippians 2:9).

This picture of a man on the throne of God, which summarizes how the Nicene Creed presents the logic of Christian worship as well as the story of salvation, shows up in various forms at the center of the apostolic faith of the New Testament. Here are four forms of the picture.

First, the ancient Christian hymn that Paul quotes in Philippians 2:6–11 depicts the whole creation worshiping Jesus Christ and confessing that he is the LORD. This hymn gives us a picture of the same thing that is said in words by the primal Christian confession *Kyrios Iesous*, "Jesus is Lord." He sits on the throne of God because the name of the LORD rightly belongs to him. The whole Nicene Creed is built around this faith: that the worship given to this man is the same worship owed to the LORD, the God of Israel. The hymn makes this clear by picking up a striking little phrase from the Ten Commandments, which forbids the worship of "anything that is in heaven above, or that is in the earth beneath, *or that is in the water under the earth*" (Exodus 20:4). The hymn alludes to this prohibition of false worship by turning it around to indicate true worship, in which every knee shall bow "in heaven and on earth *and under the earth*" (Philippians 2:10). The hymn presents Christian worship today as the firstfruits of the whole creation fulfilling the requirement of worship in the Ten Commandments, which is worship of the LORD alone.

Second, in the worship depicted in the last book of the Bible, the Lamb is standing at the center of the throne in heaven (Revelation 5:6), and the voice of thousands of angels declares: "Worthy is the Lamb that was slain, to receive power and wealth and wisdom and might and honor and glory and blessing" (Revelation 5:12). And then once again we have a vision of the eschatological worship of the whole creation, as "every creature in heaven and on earth *and under the earth* and in the sea" joins in worshiping the Lord Jesus, the Lamb that was slain, with the same worship that is given to the one who sits on the throne from the beginning: "To him who sits on the throne and to the Lamb be blessing and honor and glory and might forever and ever" (Revelation 5:13). The picture here expands the one in Daniel 7:13, where the Son of Man comes on the clouds to stand before the Ancient of Days seated on the throne in heaven. And now it is as if the whole creation acclaims with joy what the LORD on the throne says to the Lord who has come to stand before him: "Sit at my right hand, until I make your enemies your footstool" (Psalm 110:1). This Lord of all is called the Lamb because he is not only the King that is enthroned but the sacrifice that was offered, as the hosts of heaven declare: "For you were slain, and by your blood you ransomed people for God from every tribe and language and people and nation" (Revelation 5:9). The result of his sacrifice is that those he has ransomed with his blood are both priests and kings with him, "and they shall reign on the earth" (Revelation 5:10).

Third, the letter to the Hebrews also relies on the picture of Jesus' incarnate presence in the highest heaven, where "after making purification for sins, he sat down at the right hand of the Majesty on high" (Hebrews 1:3; see 8:1). He is the "great high priest who has passed through the heavens" (4:14) because he has been "made higher than the heavens" (7:26, KJV). Again the picture is of a heaven above the visible heavens, a place beyond all places, an invisible dimension. For Christ our high priest did not enter into the temple on earth, which is merely a copy of the true temple above, but "into heaven itself, now to appear in the presence of God on our behalf" (9:24). The atonement he makes for sin is not completed on the cross but in the heavenly sanctuary, where he brings his own human blood to cleanse us from sin (9:12). It is of the utmost importance, therefore, that Jesus in heaven is not a disembodied soul but a living human being, flesh and blood in the presence of God. Unlike the blood of bulls and goats used to make atonement in the earthly temple, his human blood in the heavenly sanctuary cleanses our consciences (9:14). One reason we are to picture the throne of God high above the heavens is to recognize that from this height there is nothing below that escapes his view, including the poor whom he raises from the dust (Psalm 113:5–7), as well as the dark and secret places of the human heart (1 Kings 8:39), which can only be cleansed by the blood of the Lamb that was slain—the man who is both priest and sacrifice in one person.

Fourth, on the day of Pentecost, it is Jesus exalted at the right hand of God who pours out the promised Holy Spirit (Acts 2:33). Peter tells us this in his sermon explaining what has happened to make so many people give voice to the gospel in so many of the languages of the world. He quotes Psalm 110 about the LORD telling the Lord to sit at his right hand (Acts 2:34), from which he draws the conclusion: "Let all the house of Israel therefore know for certain that God has made him both Lord and Christ" (2:36). Once again the enthronement in heaven of Christ, the Son of David, is a picture of what it means to confess in words that Jesus is LORD. From his heavenly throne he guides the church by pouring out the Holy Spirit, sending his people on their mission from Jerusalem to the ends of the earth (Acts 1:8).

His heavenly throne does not mean he is absent from us on earth but signifies the presence of the right hand of God ruling in sovereign power over all things. It is a sovereignty that can be revealed when the veil of heaven is taken away, as when Jesus in heaven speaks to Paul on earth, back when he went by the name of Saul and was persecuting the church: "Saul, Saul, why are you persecuting me?" (Acts 9:4). In persecuting the Body of Christ on earth, Saul is attacking the Lord in heaven, for although Jesus' resurrected body is now free from all possibility of harm, the Body of his people, which he claims as his own, is not yet. This is one reason why the Gospels, which were written down well after Christians began worshiping the exalted Jesus in his heavenly glory, had to emphasize Jesus' commandment to follow him by taking up a cross. It is not as if the Gospel writers were starting with what scholars call a "low Christology," knowing nothing of the divinity of Christ—as if the early Christians had never heard that the LORD said to their Lord, "sit at my right hand." The Gospels were written for a community that regularly bowed the knee to the Lord Jesus and awaited his coming in glory, and therefore had to be reminded that before they sat in glory with him (Mark 10:37), they would suffer with him. So also when Jesus from heaven reveals himself to Saul on earth, his purpose included showing him "how much he must suffer for the sake of my name" (Acts 9:16).

AND SHALL COME
AGAIN IN GLORY

GLORY IS THE light of divine revelation made visible and the blessing of divine presence enjoyed. Its opposite is hiddenness and humiliation. Our Lord's second coming is not called a descent, because it is glorious. Jesus coming again is Jesus still exalted and ever-living, but now made known to all on earth. To see why the Creed speaks here of glory, it will help to recall how Jesus speaks of the scriptural witness to the Son of Man in Daniel 7, which along with Psalm 110 is the most frequently-quoted passage of Scripture in the New Testament.

In the book of Daniel, Israel is in exile, and one foreign king after another holds them in bondage, as Pharaoh once did in Egypt. In chapter 7, Daniel the Israelite dreams of great beasts which seek power and destruction, representing the kingdoms of this world that God will bring to an end. For Daniel sees also the judgment that is stored up in heaven, where one called the Ancient of Days—a name for God in his eternity—sits on a throne that is everlasting (Daniel 7:9). And then, in the crucial passage, there comes to the Ancient of Days on the clouds of heaven one like a Son of Man (Daniel 7:13), not a cruel beast but a representative of the people of God—who in turn represent all humanity—one whom both Jews and Christians can call the Son of David, the anointed King. To him is given lordship, glory, and a kingdom that has no end, so that all peoples, all nations, and all languages should serve him (Daniel 7:14), which is to say, should worship him.

The New Testament reads this passage as saying the same thing as Psalm 110, where the LORD says to our Lord, "Sit at my right hand until I make your enemies your footstool." The enemies subjected to him include all the savage kingdoms of this world, none of which lasts forever. But more than that, the enemies he defeats include all that harms and corrupts the good creation of God, including sin and suffering and finally death, which is "the last enemy to be destroyed" (1 Corinthians 15:26). This is glory.

To Judge the Living
and the Dead

$\mathcal{T}$HE THRONE OF God the Father, the Ancient of Days, is at the center of a court of judgment (Daniel 7:9–10). Jesus as the Son of Man has received from the Father authority to execute judgment (John 5:27). He died and lived so that he might be Lord both of the dead and the living (Romans 14:9), and thereby become the man "appointed by God to be judge of the living and the dead" (Acts 10:42). For "we must all appear before the judgment seat of Christ" (2 Corinthians 5:10).

The concept of a last judgment is so familiar in Western Christian culture that we may miss how unique this is. Pagan mythology tells of judges in the underworld who were once human kings like Minos and Rhadamanthus. But it knows nothing of a judgment from heaven that concerns both the living and the dead. Much less does it imagine the whole world facing the judgment of a man enthroned at the right hand of divine power—a man who was once subjected to the shameful injustice and cruelty of a cross. This is the man who promised that those who hunger and thirst for justice shall be filled, those who mourn shall be comforted, the merciful shall receive mercy, and the gentle people in this cruel world are blessed, for they shall inherit the whole earth (Matthew 5:4–7). Now he is in a position to make good on that promise.

For those of us who are less than gentle and merciful and just, there is of course reason to be afraid of this Judge, before whom we must each give an account of ourselves (Romans 14:12). And Christians in particular, who like Peter are especially tempted to avoid taking up the cross and following Christ (Mark 8:31–33), have reason to fear that the Son of Man will be ashamed of us "when he comes in the glory of his Father with the holy angels" (Mark 8:38). For us too the preaching of the gospel must begin with the word "repent," for the kingdom of heaven is at hand (Matthew 3:2). Yet this is a good word, for to Peter came also the promise of this same Judge that sins absolved in his name on earth are absolved in heaven as well (Matthew 16:19). So in the end, we should await the coming of the Lord knowing that we shall find salvation in him (Hebrews 9:28). For it is through his judgment that the kingdom of our Father comes to be on earth as it is in heaven, just as we have been asking all along (Matthew 6:10).

Of Whose Kingdom
There Shall Be No End

THE SON OF MAN coming on the clouds of heaven to the Ancient of Days is given an everlasting kingdom so that all peoples, nations, and languages shall serve him (Daniel 7:14). The ambition of kings and emperors who want to devour the earth like ravenous beasts is here brought to an end (Daniel 7:1–8). In their place Jesus, the Son of Man, is given "an everlasting dominion which shall not pass away" (Daniel 7:14).

Jesus alludes to this passage when interrogated by the high priest at his trial: "From now on you will see the Son of Man seated at the right hand of Power and coming on the clouds of heaven" (Matthew 26:64). This is enough to get him crucified, for as the high priest's servants later remind Pilate, "Everyone who makes himself a king opposes Caesar" (John 19:12). Indeed, by identifying himself as the Son of Man coming on the clouds of heaven, Jesus is claiming to be not just any king but the true Son of David, of whom the LORD said, "I will establish the throne of his kingdom forever" (2 Samuel 7:13). David's throne, not Caesar's, is the one that will endure for all generations (Psalm 89:4), for only of the Son of David does God say: "I have chosen him to be my son, and I will be his father" (1 Chronicles 28:6). This good news of the "Son of the Most High," who sits "on the throne of his father David" and who will "reign over the house of Jacob forever," is one of the things the angel tells Mary at his annunciation—adding "and of his kingdom there will be no end," from which this phrase of the Creed is taken (Luke 1:32–33).

Jesus' coming in glory means that he is king forever, and not just in heaven. He sits on the throne established forever over all things, so that every knee shall bow to him not only in heaven but also on earth and even under the earth, which is to say even in the land of the dead (Philippians 2:10). People from every generation of every nation and tribe and language shall stand before the throne of the Lamb, raised from the dead, worshiping him (Revelation 7:9–10). For over the course of the ages they will have been taught to obey everything that he has commanded (Matthew 28:20). The result will be a banquet for all peoples in which he swallows up death forever and wipes all tears from their eyes (Isaiah 26:6–8).

The kingdom of heaven comes to earth as God himself dwells among the peoples in his tabernacle (Revelation 21:3), his human tent of flesh now clothed in a lasting dwelling from heaven (2 Corinthians 5:1–4), as human mortality in Christ puts on immortality (1 Corinthians 15:53). The fulfillment of God's covenant with Israel thus becomes a blessing for all the families of the earth (Genesis 12:3), as we are taught in the gospel preached beforehand to Abraham (Galatians 3:8). "I will take you to be my people and I will be your God," says the LORD to Israel (Exodus 6:7), a promise that echoes throughout the Bible in one covenant renewal after another (Jeremiah 31:33, Ezekiel 36:26–28, 37:26–27) down to the last chapters, when God pitches his tent among all the children of Adam so that all of them "will be his people, and God himself will be with them as their God" (Revelation 21:3).

Jesus Christ, the only-begotten Son of God, the Son of David who is enthroned as the Son of Man on high, is our Lord who sits at the right hand of the LORD until all enemies are put under his feet, including death itself (1 Corinthians 15:25–26). This is the life of the age to come, to which the Creed shall return at the end.

ARTICLE 3

THE HOLY
SPIRIT

And in the Holy Spirit

Earlier translations call him "the Holy Ghost," because "ghost" is an old word for "spirit." Almost five hundred years ago, when the *Book of Common Prayer* (the prayerbook of the Church of England) made "Holy Ghost" into a standard English term, the prayerbook could also speak of "ghostly counsel," meaning "spiritual counsel." Shakespeare and his friends would have understood. But for us it takes a bit of adjustment. The most important adjustment is to connect "spirit" with life and power, not death or the underworld or a forlorn, merely spiritual existence. In both the Old Testament and New Testament, "spirit" contrasts with "flesh" as life-giving power contrasts with mortality, need, and vulnerability.

And this is not just any spirit, but the Spirit of the LORD, as the Old Testament puts it. Thus it is the *Holy* Spirit, uniquely set apart from all spirits in creation, and also the source and giver of holiness and sanctification (Romans 15:16). The name in Latin, *Sanctus Spiritus*, shows us the origin of the word "sanctification," which comes from *sanctus*, meaning "holy" (used of a person, it means "saint"). Thus to sanctify is to make holy, to hallow or consecrate. At the same time, the word "spirit" (*ruach* in Hebrew, *pneuma* in Greek, *spiritus* in Latin), which in all three languages can also mean "breath," suggests a uniquely intimate relationship with the life in all creatures. We keep finding the Holy Spirit *within* creatures, like the breath of life that is in them.

In the original Creed of the Council of Nicaea in 325, the Creed came to an end here with the words "and in the Holy Spirit." This led to a problem, because the question arose: Should we say the Holy Spirit is just as fully God as Christ is, and that like Christ he is *homoousios* with the Father? The view that prevailed in the Council of Constantinople in 381 was a clear *yes*. But the Nicene Creed of 381, the Creed we are now studying, did not say so—not in so many words. This evidently frustrated some of the most important members of the Council, including Gregory Naziansen, who was firmly in favor of saying the Holy Spirit was fully God and *homoousios* with the Father and the Son. It seems that this Creed was originally presented in the Council as a kind of compromise document, in the hope that those who hesitated to say this about the Holy Spirit could still be united with the rest of the church that confessed the faith of Nicaea. In the end, however, they walked out of the Council without accepting its new version of the Creed.[31] This is hardly surprising, for as we are about to see, the phrases this Creed adds after "in the Holy Spirit" amount to a clear confession that the Holy Spirit cannot be anything other than God, the Creator rather than a creature, having the same divine essence as the Father and the Son.

THE LORD

T HE CREED HERE is based on Paul's saying that "the Lord is the Spirit" (2 Corinthians 3:17). To put the word "Lord" here means using the same word of the Spirit that is used of Christ, even after confessing Christ as the "one Lord." The logic of it is just like calling Christ "God from God," even after confessing faith in "one God, the Father." We are saying we believe in one God, the Father, and that Christ also is God. And we are saying we believe in one Lord, Jesus Christ, and that the Spirit also is the Lord. At this point we have the gist of the doctrine labeled "Trinity." (For the puzzling arithmetic of this, which is genuinely puzzling but is not the really important mystery of the Trinity, see the Epilogue.)

To say the Holy Spirit is the Lord is to make it impossible to say he is merely an angel, as some theologians of the time wanted to say. It also makes it impossible to say that he is simply the energy of God working within us, or an aspect or attribute or quality of God. The Spirit of the LORD is not just a name for the presence of the LORD in us, for he is the LORD himself, a distinct being different from the Father. We need a word for this, and the theologians who prevailed at Constantinople used the Greek term *hypostasis*. As used by the Nicene tradition from then on, this means a complete individual being. You and I are both *hypostases* (plural of *hypostasis*), but our hands and feet are not. So the Holy Spirit is Lord and God, not a part of God or an aspect of God or the working or presence of God. Thus the Nicene tradition came to speak of God as three *hypostases*—Father, Son, and Holy Spirit—which in Latin became three *subsistentiae*, and in English three "subsistences." This is simply an abstract term for three complete individual beings of any kind—not parts or aspects, energies or activities of some other being.

Another term was also used: *prosopon* in Greek, which is *persona* in Latin, from which we get the English word "person." This becomes the most common word used by the Western tradition for what there is three of in God. Most English-speaking Christians have heard God described as "three persons." In large part as a result of the presence of Nicene theology, "persons" came to be a weighty and important term in Western thought—so much so that we need to be aware of the very limited sense in which it is used in Nicene theology. At the time the Nicene Creed was written, *persona* and *prosopon* were not important philosophical terms for describing human beings. They were not used to refer to anyone's "personality," a modern word for which there is no real equivalent in Greek or Latin (the closest equivalent would be words designating someone's ethical *character*, whether they were vicious or virtuous). If you wanted to think about what makes us human, you would talk about body and soul, mind and reason, not personality or "personhood" (another very modern word). The very notion of personhood, so important in modern thought, is a kind of gift given to Western culture by the Nicene doctrine of the Trinity—which has become so rich a gift that it must be used with caution when speaking of Father, Son, and Holy Spirit.

According to Nicene theology there are not three personalities in God—as if God were a trio of friends like Mary and John and Peter—for there is but one God, having one will and power and activity, as well as one essence or *ousia*.

Nicene theology after the Council of Constantinople in 381 uses terms like "person" to make the very abstract term *hypostasis* a bit more specific. Dogs and cats are *hypostases*, since they are complete individual beings (not just ears or tails). But they are not persons, for they are not *rational* beings with language, logic, and reason (*logos*). They do not fit the definition of "person" that prevailed in Western theology for over a thousand years: "An individual substance of rational nature" (where "individual substance" is another way of saying *hypostasis*).[32]

If all this still sounds abstract, it is. To speak *concretely* of the Holy Trinity is to speak of Father, Son, and Holy Spirit, as explained in the Epilogue. The abstract language has its uses in clarifying some logical issues, such as the fact that the Holy Spirit is not part of God (for God has no parts, and the Holy Spirit is God, not part of God). But the real root and life of the Nicene doctrine of the Trinity is not talk of persons or *hypostases* but worship of the God in whose name we are baptized: the Father, the Son, and the Holy Spirit.

AND GIVER OF LIFE

"GIVER OF LIFE" is one word in Greek: *zoopoion*, literally "Lifemaker," the one who makes alive.[33] This too is a way of saying that the Holy Spirit is God, doing what only God can do. For the Spirit of God does not receive life as living creatures do, but only gives life, which is what the Creator alone does. Hence Jesus' human life begins in Mary's womb by the power of the Holy Spirit, as we have seen, and so also his human life is restored in the resurrection by the Holy Spirit, for he was "put to death in the flesh but made alive in the spirit" (1 Peter 3:18). In Romans 8—a chapter that is all about contrasting life in the Spirit with death in the flesh—Paul shows how the resurrected life of Christ becomes ours, using the verb *zoopoein* ("to give life" or "make alive"): "If the Spirit of him who raised Jesus from the dead dwells in you, he who raised Christ Jesus from the dead will also *give life* to your mortal bodies through the Spirit who dwells in you" (Romans 8:11). The Father gives everlasting life through the Spirit, beginning with the humanity of Jesus, who lays down his life but also has authority to take it up again (John 10:18). Hence the resurrection is the work of the whole Trinity—Father, Son, and Holy Spirit—all giving life to the human flesh of Jesus.

The Spirit must give life, for the flesh accomplishes nothing, says Jesus (John 6:63). He is talking about *our* flesh, because *his* flesh, he says, is living bread from heaven, given for the life of the world (John 6:51). It is life-giving flesh, the church father Cyril of Alexandria teaches, because it is the flesh of God incarnate, through which the Spirit of God gives us everlasting life.[34] Only the human flesh of Christ can both receive divine life and give it, for this alone is God's own flesh; it is the true temple in heaven (Hebrews 8:2), the place in creation where the life-giving energy of the Spirit is most powerfully at work. This again is the work of the one God, Father, Son, and Holy Spirit, whose work is always one work, never divided or separated.

WHO PROCEEDS FROM
THE FATHER

OUR LORD TEACHES that the Holy Spirit is "the Spirit of truth, who proceeds from the Father" (John 15:26). "Procession" thus becomes a technical term in Trinitarian theology, used for the origination of the Spirit from the Father, which is a different origination from the begetting of the Son. Unfortunately (and here we shall have to get technical for a moment), because of the shortage of biblical vocabulary, "procession" is also used in a more generic sense to refer to both originations. So the begetting of the Son is one divine procession and the procession of the Spirit is another. Each procession is unique—they are not two of the same kind—for the Father begets only one Son and has only one Spirit. We don't have a biblical term for the unique kind of origination by which the Spirit proceeds from the Father, so the only distinctive word we have for this is a made-up term, "spiration." Thus theologians sometimes find it helpful to say: the Father begets the Son but spirates the Spirit.

Rather more helpful is the distinction between processions and missions. "Mission" comes from the Latin *missio*, which means sending (missionaries are people *sent* on a mission). The Spirit *proceeds* eternally from the Father but is *sent* to us by the Son at the right hand of God (Acts 2:33). So "mission," in this technical sense, is the sending of the Holy Spirit into the world and into our hearts. The Son too is sent (John 3:17), and thus has a mission from the Father. So "mission" or sending, in Trinitarian theology, refers to things that happen at a specific time and place in the world, involving creatures affected by the work of God, whereas "procession" refers not to creatures at all but to the life of God in eternity, as for example in the eternal begetting of the Son.

Through the working of God in the missions, we can see something about order in the processions. As the Nicene fathers put it, every work of God originates with the Father, is given to the Son, and is completed by the Holy Spirit. This is true also of the very being (*ousia*) of God: it originates with the Father, is given to the Son, and is completed by the Holy Spirit. For this reason also we speak of the Father as the first person of the Trinity, the Son as the second person, and the Holy Spirit as the third person: all equally divine, but ordered according to the processions by which they originate from the Father. This labeling—first person, second person, third person—is inevitable also because of the Creed's roots in baptismal confession. We are baptized in the name of the Father, the Son, and the Holy Spirit, not "in the name of the Holy Spirit, and of the Son, and of the Father."

[And from the Son]

THIS PHRASE IS the tragic difference between the Latin and Greek versions of the Creed that was mentioned in the Introduction. It is one word in Latin, *filioque*, which was added to the Creed in the West without any consultation with the East. The addition originated from local usage in Spain in the sixth century and gradually spread to the rest of the Western world.[35] The Eastern Orthodox churches have never accepted it as part of the Creed, and they have a point. The Creed should not be expanded except by an ecumenical council in which all branches of the church participate. What's more, putting something in the Creed implies that it is essential to the Nicene faith, and there is no good reason for thinking that you have to accept this added phrase in order to be a sound Nicene Christian.

Here we enter into controversial territory, and what I am about to say should be heard for what it is: the view of a Western Christian who thinks what the *filioque* is meant to say is something that is true but not essential to the Nicene faith, and therefore does not belong in the Creed. It is, to use another technical term, a *theologoumenon*: a theological proposition that many of us think is true, but which is not a teaching that you have to believe in order to be a faithful Christian. We can affirm its truth while also insisting that it is in a very important sense optional. Therefore it should not remain in the Creed, and like many Western theologians who think this way, I do not say the words "and of the Son" when I recite the Creed.

On the other hand, I do not think this phrase is teaching heresy or false doctrine. For one thing, the phrase is so brief that its meaning needs to be spelled out, and one possible interpretation is that the Spirit proceeds from the Father through the Son, which is a formulation to which the Eastern Orthodox have no objection. Still, the *theologoumenon* the phrase is intended to express says more than this, and

I should tell you a bit about what that is. It is a doctrine called "double procession," which says that the Father and the Son are together the source from which the Spirit proceeds. The doctrine was developed and defended by the great Western church father Augustine, and his presentation is the standard account of it. His fundamental reason for thinking it's true is that the Spirit is the Spirit of the Son as well as of the Father. With the concerns of the Eastern Orthodox in mind, we can note two further points in Augustine's teaching.

First, Augustine teaches that the Son is not a separate source or principle of the Spirit, as if he were operating independently of the Father. Rather, Father and Son are together one source of the Spirit. Moreover, the fact that the Son *can* be this one source together with the Father is itself a power that he receives wholly from the Father, for the Son receives all things from the Father—everything that he has and is. Conversely, the Father gives everything that is his to the Son, except being Father. So one of the things the Son receives from the Father is the power to be that from which the Spirit proceeds.[36]

Second—as we can see from the first point—Augustine is very careful to uphold the truth that the Father is the source of all that is divine. Later Western theology reinforces this, as for example when the Council of Toledo in 675 teaches that the Father is the *fons et origo totius divinitatis*, the source and origin of all that is divine. There was a time when some theologians had the notion that Augustine's version of the Trinity "starts with" the one divine essence (*ousia*) rather than with God the Father, but this is nonsense which Augustine scholarship today has thoroughly debunked. Augustine starts at the same place as the Creed and all the Nicene fathers, locating the origin of all that is divine in God the Father. It is from the Father that the divine essence comes to the Son and the Spirit. The divine essence does not beget anything and is not a source of anything. To speak thus would be a piece of bad grammar, like saying human nature begets a child or gives birth. Only fathers and mothers do that, though they do it *by virtue of* their human nature. And so we can say that the Father begets the Son by virtue of his divine nature, giving him the whole of his divine essence, and that the Spirit, who also is *homoousios* with the Father, proceeds from the Father by virtue of receiving the same divine essence.

Who with the Father and Son Together Is Worshiped and Co-Glorified

WITH APOLOGIES, I am presenting an awkward and unusual translation of this phrase in order to highlight something that is unusual and hard to translate: the repetition of the Greek word *syn*, meaning "with" or "together." It's a word that appears, in slight variation, in many English words derived from Greek, such as *syn*thesis (putting one thing *together with* another), *sym*phony (making music *together with* others), and *sym*pathy (feeling another person's emotions together *with* her). In this phrase of the Creed it appears three times, first as a preposition (*"with* the Father"), then as an adverb (*"together"*), and finally as a prefix (*co*-glorified). The repetition is worth highlighting because it is a way of emphasizing the inseparability of the Father, the Son, and the Holy Spirit as one God, which is evident in the fact that they are rightly worshiped with one another, co-glorified together with equal and inseparable honor.

With this emphasis on worship the Creed comes to the point that was always the fundamental basis of the doctrine of the Trinity. As we are baptized in the name of the Father, the Son, and the Holy Spirit, so we worship the Father, the Son, and the Holy Spirit as our God, the one Creator of heaven and earth—which means we cannot possibly regard the Father, the Son, and the Holy Spirit as unequal in any way, as if any one of them deserved a lower and lesser worship than the others. And yet neither does Christian faith allow this worship to be given to more than one God. The logic of Christian worship is thus the logic of the Nicene faith. It took a while, but with ancient Christian practices of worship in view, the triumph of Nicene theology looks inevitable in retrospect. It is theology catching up with what Christians have always believed when they worship.

WHO HAS SPOKEN
THROUGH THE PROPHETS

W HEN THE PROPHETS of Israel say, "Thus says the LORD," it is the Holy Spirit who speaks through them. David the king is speaking as a prophet when he says, "The Spirit of the LORD speaks by me, his word is on my tongue" (2 Samuel 23:2). The apostle Peter says as much when he tells the other apostles of what "the Holy Spirit spoke beforehand by the mouth of David" (Acts 1:16). Likewise when the apostle Paul quotes a passage from the prophet Isaiah, he describes it as what the Holy Spirit said (Acts 28:25), and the letter to the Hebrews introduces a quotation from the Psalms by saying, "as the Holy Spirit says" (Hebrews 3:7).

And that is just the beginning. Plainly the apostles think that when they quote the prophets, the Holy Spirit is speaking *today.* This is why after Scripture is read to a congregation, it is appropriate to conclude by saying: "The word of the Lord." Moreover, there are prophets in the New Testament church (Acts 13:1, 21:9–10). Indeed, whenever the book of Acts notes that people are "filled with the Spirit," we are about to hear them utter prophetic speech authorized by God (Acts 2:4, 4:8, 4:31, 13:9; see 11:28). Likewise at the beginning of the Gospel of Luke, when Elizabeth is filled with the Spirit she greets Mary as "the mother of my Lord" (Luke 1:41–43). When her husband is filled with the Spirit his tongue is loosed and he utters one of the great inspired prayers of the Bible (Luke 1:67–79). And when their son John the Baptist is filled with the Spirit in his mother's womb (Luke 1:15), it is as if he's practicing for his later task as a prophet, leaping for joy at the coming of Jesus in Mary's womb (Luke 1:41).

The Holy Spirit, the Giver of Life, gives us everlasting life mainly by giving us divine words. For it is Christ who is our life (Colossians 3:4), and he is given to us by the word of God, which is in turn given to us by the Spirit inspiring all who testify to Christ in the Scriptures, for he is the Spirit of Truth who guides them into all truth (John 16:13). The New Testament describes Scripture (2 Timothy 3:16) as divinely inspired or "God-breathed,"[37] adding that it is profitable for teaching, for reproof and correction, and for education in justice (2 Timothy 3:6). Above all, says Jesus, the Holy Spirit "will bear witness about me" (John 15:26) and "will glorify me" (John 16:14), thus completing the work of the Trinity, for "all that the Father has is mine, and therefore I said that he [the Holy Spirit] will take what is mine and declare it to you" (John 16:15).

Christ is ours by faith, which comes by hearing, which comes by the word of Christ (Romans 10:17), which comes by the Holy Spirit inspiring prophets and apostles and their testimony in holy Scripture, as well as all teaching and preaching and singing that draws its life from this inspired testimony. Thus when the apostle bids a congregation to "*be filled with the Spirit*, addressing one another in psalms and hymns and spiritual songs" (Ephesians 5:18–19), this is another way of saying what he has to say in a parallel passage: "*Let the word of Christ dwell in you richly*, teaching and admonishing one another in all wisdom, singing psalms and hymns and spiritual songs"

(Colossians 3:16). To be filled with the Spirit is to have the word of Christ dwelling richly in the congregation. Word and Spirit thus go together. This is why the apostle tells us that no one can confess that "Jesus is Lord" except by the Holy Spirit (1 Corinthians 12:3). The word of God apart from the Spirit of God falls on deaf ears and stirs up no faith in our hearts. And the connection goes both ways: if the Holy Spirit had not given us the word of Christ through prophets and apostles, we would have no Christ to believe in and therefore no faith to confess, and the Spirit of Christ himself would be far from our hearts. In this way faith itself, along with Christ whom we receive by faith and the Spirit who stirs up our faith, is the gift of God.

In One, Holy, Catholic, and Apostolic Church

$\mathfrak{L}$IKE THE SECOND article, the third article of the Creed can be split into two parts. As the dividing point of the second article is when it turns from Christ's divinity to his humanity, the dividing point of the third article is when it turns from the divine being of the Holy Spirit to his work among us human beings. The central place of his working is the church, the Body of Christ. He is the Spirit of Christ's Body, giving it life in Christ through the word of the gospel. There is no spiritual life for Christians apart from this Body, any more than a human hand or eye can be a living hand or eye apart from a living human body (1 Corinthians 12:21). Separated from the life of the Body, we are separated from Christ, its head; we wither and die like branches cut off from a vine (John 15:16). For all the spiritual gifts of Christians are given not for private use but for the building up of the Body of Christ (Ephesians 4:12).

The Creed describes the Body of Christ with four adjectives, which have come to be called the four distinctive "marks" of the church.

First, the church is *one*, because "we, though many, are one body in Christ" (Romans 12:5). It is one Body with one head, Jesus Christ, from which all the members are nourished and knit together and grow into something glorious (Colossians 2:19), drawing their life from Christ himself like branches of one vine (John 15:5), sharing a variety of gifts but one Spirit (Ephesians 4:4).

Second, the church is *holy*, set apart for Christ alone, and thus sanctified by the Holy Spirit. Though hardly perfect, this is the community which the Lord himself is making perfect by the gift of his Spirit, so that in the end he may present her to himself as a glorious bride, his own forever, spotless and holy (Ephesians 5:26–27).

Third, the church is *catholic*, which comes from a Greek term meaning "universal." There are many local congregations of the Body of Christ, but only one Body throughout the world. So the church's catholicity is a result of its unity. Because heretics break off from this unity and create divisions and factions (1 Corinthians 11:18–19), "catholic" has also come to have the secondary meaning of "orthodox," from a Greek term for sound faith and teaching. To say a teaching is catholic, small "c," is the same as saying it is orthodox.

Fourth, the church is *apostolic*, because the gospel by which we are saved (1 Corinthians 15:1–2) is the faith that God gave to the world through the preaching of the apostles. As the apostle Paul says: "So we preached and so you believed" (1 Corinthians 15:11). Since the apostles' preaching, like the words of the prophets of old, now comes to us in holy Scripture, calling the church "apostolic" is the Creed's way of saying it is biblical. The faith of the church is the gift of the Holy Spirit who inspired both prophets and apostles and thus all of Scripture for our learning and for the building up of the Body of Christ.

WE CONFESS ONE BAPTISM
FOR THE FORGIVENESS OF SINS

THE WORD "BAPTISM" is derived from a Greek word meaning to dip or dunk, which can be used to describe dipping your finger into a bit of water (Luke 16:24) or a morsel of food into a sauce (John 13:16). To be baptized is to be dipped or immersed in water in the name of the Father, the Son, and the Holy Spirit, in accordance with our Lord's command and institution (Matthew 28:19).

The proper verb in this phrase is "confess," not merely "acknowledge," as in some translations. In Greek and also in Latin, it is the same word that is used for confessing the Creed or confessing the faith. We have already seen, back in the discussion of "We believe," how confessing the faith is rooted in baptismal confession. The Creed here, in an act of reflection, makes the baptismal confession itself into an article of faith, something to believe in. To believe in Christ includes believing in baptism in the name of the Father, the Son, and the Holy Spirit, and to confess the faith of Christ is to confess that the baptismal confession is a confession of the true faith.

There is only one baptism because there is one holy catholic church throughout the world based on the faith taught by the apostles. The apostle Paul makes the fundamental connection when he speaks of "one Lord, one faith, one baptism" (Ephesians 4:5). The one church has one faith because it has only the one Lord in whom to believe and be baptized. Whoever believes is to be baptized (Mark 16:16) so as to be buried with Christ and raised with him (Colossians 2:12) to walk in newness of life with him (Romans 6:4). It is the same baptism wherever it is the same Lord—so it is one baptism, not a different baptism in different churches, as if different congregations of the one Body of Christ each had a different head.

The Creed connects baptism with the forgiveness of sins because it connects baptism with Christ. Baptism is an initiation rite, marking the day we fully become members of the Body, belonging to Christ rather than Adam (Romans 5:12). The ancient practice of baptism, as we saw in the discussion of "We believe," resembled a ceremony in which you were inducted into the army. To be baptized was like renouncing your old life as a civilian and committing yourself instead to sharing the responsibilities, tasks, and dangers of a soldier who belongs to Christ for the rest of your days. But this also means sharing in the grace of Christ, his resurrection, and the forgiveness of sins. For not only is our old life buried with Christ in baptism, but we receive a new life, being raised with him through faith in the working of God (Colossians 2:12). Hence Scripture calls baptism a "washing of rebirth" and connects it with "the renewal of the Holy Spirit" (Titus 3:5). In this new life in Christ, we become partakers of all that belongs to him, including the forgiveness of sins, justification, sanctification, redemption, and everlasting life (1 Corinthians 1:30). Baptism does not provide some kind of automatic guarantee, of course, any more than induction into the army guarantees you will be a good soldier. But it is the indispensable beginning, which marks you for life.

WE LOOK FOR THE
RESURRECTION OF THE DEAD

IN HIS RESURRECTION our Lord Jesus is "the firstfruits of those who have fallen asleep" (1 Corinthians 15:20), the beginning of a harvest that will include all who now "sleep in the dust of the ground" (Daniel 12:2), like seeds in the earth (John 12:24, 1 Corinthians 15:36–37). For as in Adam all die, even so in Christ shall all be made alive (1 Corinthians 15:22). Jesus' resurrection is the defeat of death, the last enemy, which the LORD puts under the feet of our Lord, as promised in Psalm 110:1 (see 1 Corinthians 15:25–26). This is not merely life after death but the undoing of death. Like our Lord, we shall not be ghosts but living human beings. For in ascending to heaven he did not leave his flesh behind, as if his incarnation had come to an end. As the angels told his disciples when they stood looking up into heaven after him: he shall come again the same way he went (Acts 1:11), which is to say, still in flesh, as the Son of Man on the clouds of heaven which signify his glory (Acts 1:9). This is the flesh of our high priest with the power of an indestructible life (Hebrews 7:16), for it is the flesh of God himself; and it is the guarantee that our resurrection too shall be to life everlasting, a resurrection of flesh that dies no more, for it is given life by the life-giving flesh of Christ.

We look for this in expectation, awaiting it in hope. It is hope for what we do not yet see (Romans 8:24), for our life is presently hidden with Christ in God (Colossians 3:3) and what we truly are does not yet appear to the human eye. But we know that when he appears from heaven, we shall be like him (1 John 3:2). We shall not be disembodied souls but living human beings clothed in everlasting life. The apostle teaches us that this corruptible flesh of ours will put on incorruption like a garment, and this mortal body will be clothed in Christ's immortality (1 Corinthians 15:53). As we have seen, the "corruption" we are preserved from is named by a Greek term that can refer to anything that gets ruined or diseased, or rots and decays like a body in the grave. So the resurrection of the flesh is the overcoming of all corruption and the healing of all harms. For in this earthly tent of corruptible flesh we now groan with desire for the incorruptible dwelling prepared in heaven for us (2 Corinthians 5:1–5), hidden with Christ at the right hand of God. We long not to be unclothed but to be clothed in the glory of this heavenly dwelling, which is to descend with Christ for us, so that what is mortal may be swallowed up by life.

AND THE LIFE OF THE
AGE TO COME

THE CREED USES this phrase as equivalent to the more compact biblical phrase that regularly gets translated "everlasting life." "Everlasting" renders the Greek adjective *aionios*, which is based on the Greek noun *aion*, meaning "age." This noun gets into English (via Latin) as the familiar word *aeon*. So "everlasting life," if we were to translate it hyper-literally, is something like "the life of ages" or "the life of aeons." What the phrase specifically refers to is the age that begins when Christ is revealed in the glory of his everlasting kingdom. In that new *aeon*, the age that is to come, we receive from our Lord a life that is *aionios*, everlasting throughout all ages (Mark 10:30).

In earlier centuries, the common translation of this phrase was "the life of the world to come." This is because four hundred years ago the English word "world" often meant "age," as we saw above.[38] "The next world" was thus an old way of saying, "the age to come," and "world without end" (used at the end of many prayers) rendered a biblical phrase that could now be translated, "for ages of ages."

The New Testament frequently contrasts "the age to come" with "this" age, which can be called "this present evil age" (Galatians 1:4), because it is the age of sin and death. "The sons of this age" (Luke 20:34) must marry and be married, for the age of death is also the age of births, as human beings need to raise families to reproduce themselves and replace the dead. But Jesus says "those who are considered worthy to attain to *that* age and to the resurrection from the dead" are different, for "they cannot die any more" (Luke 20:35–36). This is why he goes on to say that "they are equal to angels" (Luke 20:36). They are still human flesh, but they are like angels in being immortal; they are "sons of the resurrection" (Luke 20:36) and have the everlasting life of the age to come.

An age in which "death itself is no more" (Revelation 21:4) is something fundamentally and unimaginably new, and the newness affects more than just human flesh. In Christ, the Creator has become also a creature, a material being, who in his own person joins heaven and earth in everlasting peace. The rainbow in the clouds is his precursor, arching from earth to heaven and back in a sign of the covenant that the LORD makes with the earth itself and every living thing upon it (Genesis 9:13). In Christ, a new heaven and a new earth are on their way in fulfillment of this sign, for when the Creator is a creature, creation itself becomes something new. "Behold, I am making all things new," says the Lord who sits on the throne of heaven (Revelation 21:5). For the former things have passed away, all pain and sorrow and crying, and God shall wipe all tears from their eyes (Revelation 21:4). The new age of creation is when the holy city, the new Jerusalem, descends from heaven like a bride adorned in beauty for her bridegroom, so that the LORD in his tent of flesh may dwell among us and be our God, and we shall all be his people (Revelation 21:2–3). We shall see his face (Revelation 22:4), the human face of Christ transfigured, in which we shall behold the glory of God (2 Corinthians 4:6).

The life of the age to come is everlasting life, for it shares in the indestructible life of the only-begotten Son of God, whose kingdom has no end. Voices in heaven cry aloud, saying: "The kingdom of the world has become the kingdom of our Lord and of his Christ, and he shall reign forever and ever" (Revelation 11:15). The Greek here is the phrase, "for ages of ages," often translated "forever and ever" in New Testament doxologies praising the glory of God (for example, Galatians 1:5, Philippians 4:20, 1 Timothy 1:17, 1 Peter 4:11, Revelation 5:13). So all those who live in Christ shall also reign in life (Romans 5:17) as kings and queens for ages of ages (Revelation 22:5). Like the "heaven of heavens," "ages of ages" is phrasing that uses a pattern of doubling, common in Hebrew, to convey what is surpassing and superlative in degree. As the heaven of heavens is a place above and beyond all places of the world, so the ages of ages are the transcendence that surpasses all ages of time. This is what comes to us when Christ comes in glory, the Son of Man on the clouds of heaven.

AMEN

A LOVELY HEBREW WORD. It means "truth." We use it after the confession of faith to say: yes, it is so.

It can also express a desire: may it be so, let the promise be kept and come true.

Amen. Even so, come Lord Jesus.

Epilogue

The Trinity in Simple Terms

The DOCTRINE OF the Trinity is about the God in whose name we are baptized: the Father, the Son, and the Holy Spirit. The mystery it reveals has at its heart the eternal begetting of the Son and the eternal procession of the Spirit. The technical terms needed to give a precise account of the logic of the doctrine, terms like *ousia* and *hypostasis* and person, have proved to be indispensable but are not the heart of the doctrine. Still less important is talk about how God is "three in one," which is a nice piece of rhetoric but is hardly essential to the doctrine itself. The Creed never uses the word "three," and you can be a perfectly fine Nicene Christian, well-instructed in the doctrine of the Trinity, without ever having heard that God is "three in one." For that matter, the label "Trinity," as handy as it is, is not essential to the doctrine of the Trinity. What is essential is the faith in God—Father, Son, and Holy Spirit—that is confessed in the Creed. So no preacher need be flummoxed, as so often happens on Trinity Sunday, by the impossibility of explaining how God is three in one. You can teach the doctrine of the Trinity without ever bothering with the word "three."

What is helpful is to understand something of the logic of the doctrine of the Trinity. It is a *doctrine*, after all, which means it is something meant to be taught (from Latin *doctrina*, "teaching"). It has a logic; for it is not some kind of mumbo jumbo about threeness and oneness but rather the Christian teaching that *makes sense* of the way Scripture tells the story of God the Father, Jesus the Son of God, and the Holy Spirit. This logic can be stated in simple language, without technical terminology.[39]

The bare bones of the logic can be set down in seven statements, which I learned from Augustine. Once you learn them, you can teach someone the bare bones of the doctrine of the

Trinity in less than two minutes (I've done it more than once).
You start with a trio of affirmations about who is God:

1. The Father is God.

2. The Son is God.

3. The Holy Spirit is God.

Then you add a trio of negations, to distinguish each from the other (to remember how it goes, move forward from the first person to the second, then from the second to the third, and come back at the end to the first person):

4. The Father is not the Son.

5. The Son is not the Holy Spirit.

6. The Holy Spirit is not the Father.

Then, for the clincher, add monotheism:

7. There is only one God.

As you can see, the word "three" is not needed, but the word "one" is essential. Pagans can say Jupiter is a god and Venus is a god and Apollo is a god, but they end up with three gods. The doctrine of the Trinity is different, because it literally doesn't add up. You could say it has a logic without arithmetic (which, it turns out, is fairly common in modern formal logic). It is a logic that makes sense of the way the Bible tells stories about God: how Christ the Son, for example, sits at the right hand of the Father and pours out the Holy Spirit on Pentecost (Acts 2:33). Or how it is that we can say God died on a cross (for the Son is God) but not that the Father died (for the Father is not the Son).

Of course there is a lot more to say about the Trinity than just these seven statements. This is just the logical bare bones. To put flesh on these bones you need to do things like teach the Creed and preach the gospel and tell the story of God as Scripture tells it. Still, there is a lot packed into the bare bones logic, which can be brought out by indicating where the technical terms come in. Suppose you were to ask a question about statement 2, wondering whether Jesus, the Son, is really God just the same way the Father is. The *homoousios* is there in the Creed to give a clear answer to that question: yes, the Son is God in exactly the same sense as the Father, having the same divine being or essence as the Father. Or suppose you have someone wondering if Jesus is part of God. You could point out that according to the second statement he is not part of God; he *is* God. And likewise the Holy Spirit is not part of God or an aspect of God; he *is* God. Each person of the Trinity is a complete individual being, a *hypostasis*. The technical terms here clarify matters by ruling out certain misunderstandings.

If you're not prone to such misunderstandings, however, the seven simple statements are clear enough. You don't need a lot of technical vocabulary or fancy wording to get the bare bones of it. The important terms are the words "God," "one," and, most important of all, the threefold name in which we are baptized: the Father, the Son, and the Holy Spirit. With a little help from the Creed, you can then see how the doctrine of the Trinity includes slight variations on the threefold name that are found throughout the Bible and Christian worship. For example, when we come to the end of a time of teaching, confession, and praise, we may conclude with words of blessing such as: "The grace of the Lord Jesus Christ, the love of God, and the fellowship of the Holy Spirit be with you all" (2 Corinthians 13:14).

Notes

Prayer on pages xi is adapted from the collect for the first Sunday in Epiphany, *The Book of Common Prayer*, 1979.

1. For the history of the creeds, I follow J. N. D. Kelly's classic study, *Early Christian Creeds*, 3rd ed. (Continuum, 1972), here chapter 4.
2. On the complicated history of the text and its use in the Council of Constantinople, see Kelly, *Creeds*, chapter 10.
3. For the Greek text of the Nicene Creed of 381, I use Kelly, *Creeds*, 297. For the Greek text of the Creed of Nicaea in 325, I use Kelly, *Creeds*, 215.
4. To be precise, the East used the Greek verb for "believe" in the first-person plural, and the West used the Latin verb for "believe" in the first-person singular.
5. Kelly gives more details in *Creeds*, chapter 2.
6. So we hear from Ambrose, the bishop of Milan in the late fourth century (see Kelly, *Creeds*, 36–37).
7. This is from a set of questions in an early third-century document, the *Apostolic Tradition*, ascribed to Hippolytus (see Kelly, *Creeds*, 45–46, 90–92).
8. For example, Deuteronomy 10:14; 1 Kings 8:27; Psalm 148:4; and Nehemiah 9:6. Some translations render this phrase, "the highest heaven."

9. The word "creature" is originally a theological term desig-
    nating anything God creates, and will always be used in that
    sense in this book.

10. This insight is packed into the oft-cited Latin adage, *corruptio
    optimi pessima est,* "the corruption of the best thing is the
    worst thing."

11. That the worship of Jesus is not a later development is shown
    decisively by Richard Bauckham, *Jesus and the God of Israel*
    (Eerdmans, 2008).

12. C. S. Lewis has a very instructive discussion of this in the
    second edition of his *Studies in Words* (Cambridge University
    Press, 1967), chapter 9.

13. It may be that the aim was simply to produce the elegant
    Latin phrase, *Filium Dei unigenitum et ex Patre natum,* "the
    Son of God, only-begotten and born of the Father."

14. This startling phrase may have been inspired by the ancient
    Latin (Vulgate) translation of Psalm 110:3, "From the womb
    before the morning star I begot you" (*ex utero ante luciferum
    genui te*).

15. Those who want to track this vocabulary closely will notice
    that scholars sometimes present this word with a different
    ending: *homoousion.* This differs from *homoousios* the same
    way that "him" differs from "he"—it is in the accusative rather
    than the nominative case. This is a purely grammatical differ-
    ence, not a difference in meaning, and we can ignore it.

16. This is from the Latin confession of faith known as *Quicunque
    vult* (from its opening words) or "The Athanasian Creed." The
    latter name is misleading, however; we don't in fact know its
    author, but it is certainly not derived from the Greek church

father Athanasius. The theology is downstream from the Latin church father Augustine.

17. This is my translation, rendering two occurrences of *egeneto* with "came to be," in order to make it easier to track the vocabulary.

18. The word "Son" is added by many translations after "only-begotten" in this verse, but there is no word for "Son" here in the Greek.

19. Aquinas, *Summa Theologica*, part I, question 4, article 3, reply 4.

20. Augustine, *On Christian Doctrine*, trans. D. W. Robertson (Macmillan, 1958) 1:12.12. For a full treatment of this theme of the descent of the omnipresent God in the incarnation, see Augustine's Letter 137, which is in effect his treatise on the incarnation.

21. For a helpful guide to ancient Hebrew terminology for "flesh," "soul," "spirit," "heart," etc., see Hans Walter Wolff, *Anthropology of the Old Testament*, rev. ed. (SCM Press, 2012).

22. From Gregory's treatise "To Ablabius, On 'Not Three Gods,'" my translation.

23. My translation. "Lowliness" renders the same word that can also be translated "humility" or "humiliation."

24. Gregory Naziansen, Oration 29:19 (also known as the Third Theological Oration). I find this one of the most helpful formulations in all the church fathers for understanding the logic of the incarnation.

25. Gregory Naziansen, Letter 101.

26. This is one of the most striking insights of this great church father, which can be found in his *Scholia on the Incarnation*, §35, translated in John McGuckin, *Saint Cyril of Alexandria*

and the Christological Controversy (St. Vladimir's Seminary Press, 2004), 332–33.

27. Plato, Phaedo 64c.

28. Psalm 88:5, in the ancient Greek translation still used in the Orthodox churches. This phrase occurs in older English translations as well, such as the King James Version.

29. My translation.

30. The Apostles' Creed uses the Latin term infernum (or in some version of the text, inferos, meaning those who are below); the root of the word is the same as "inferior." It is the place of the dead in "the lower parts of the earth" (Ephesians 4:9).

31. See Kelly, Creeds, chapter 10.

32. This definition of "person" is formulated in the early 6th century by Boethius, the most important logician of the patristic era, in his Theological Tractates 5.3, with the doctrine of the Trinity very much in view. It is referred to frequently by later Western theologians such as Thomas Aquinas.

33. The zoo- here comes from the same word as "zoological gardens"—a garden for studying living creatures ("zoo" for short).

34. This is the teaching in the 11th anathema attached to Cyril's third letter to Nestorius. For translation and Cyril's own commentary, see McGuckin, Saint Cyril of Alexandria, 275.

35. The basic story is told by Kelly, Creeds, chapter 11.

36. For key discussions of this point, see Augustine, On the Trinity 4:20.29 and 15:26.47.

37. The Greek term, theopneustos, is derived from the same root as the word for "breath" or "spirit" (pneuma), which is also part of the name, "Holy Spirit." The same connection is visi-

ble in the way the English word "inspiration" is derived from the word "spirit."

38. See the discussion of "who was begotten of the Father before all ages," as well as C. S. Lewis' explanations in *Studies in Words*.

39. Here I am repeating an explanation I gave in *Good News for Anxious Christians* (Brazos Press, 2010), 184–87, as well as *The Meaning of Protestant Theology* (Baker Academic, 2020), 312–14. But it's not really my explanation, because I learned it from passages in Augustine, especially *On the Trinity* 8:1.1 and *On Christian Doctrine* 1:4.5.

Subject Index

Scripture Index

Old Testament

New Testament

CHRISTIAN ESSENTIALS

The Christian Essentials series passes down tradition that matters. The ancient church was founded on basic biblical teachings and practices like the Ten Commandments, baptism, the Apostles' Creed, the Lord's Supper, the Lord's Prayer, and corporate worship. These basics of the Christian life have sustained and nurtured every generation of the faithful—from the apostles to today. The books in the Christian Essentials series open up the meaning of the foundations of our faith.